Frontspiece:
"Godshill" by George E. Alexander, R.A.

GW00597267

A HISTORY OF GODSHILL CHURCH, VILLAGE and PARISH

Edited Selections from the Writings of
J. VINCENT JENKINS
(formerly of Church Hill, Godshill)

Overall Editor: The Revd Fr Michael Stone

Local Editors: The Revd Fr John Ryder, SSC, Ralph Abbott Esq.

Proof-reader: Dr Paul Tolley

Published by All Saints Church Godshill
on the Isle of Wight in the Year of our Lord 2013

ISBN: 978-0-9576926-0-2
Published by ALL SAINTS CHURCH GODSHILL
Printed by SHORT RUN PRESS LTD

JOHN VINCENT JENKINS (1907-2000)

JVJ was born and spent his boyhood in the Rhondda Valley of South Wales. At twenty he went some miles east to Teacher Training College at Caerleon, before launching his career many miles east in 1929 in the south of Essex. There he married Millicent and there too their two daughters Esme and Margaret were born. The surviving group photographs of this first part of his life involved Football, Cricket and Athletics, and many show JVJ as captain, as he was of Tilbury Football Club.

Apart from some special teaching responsibilities during the war with evacuee children in Norfolk, JVJ was to remain part of the School-teaching scene in Essex for forty years. He became Head-teacher of a Primary Boys School in Hornchurch from 1943 to 1950, and of Moulsham Secondary School for Boys at Chelmsford from then till his retirement in Summer 1969. Both he and Millicent were well-known in the county for their involvement in community life. JVJ rose to senior rank in both his Rotary Club and his Lodge, and Millicent served with distinction in the WRVS.

When it came time to plan their retirement, they decided to break away completely, and searched the Isle of Wight for their new home. They had no hesitation when a bungalow in Godshill came to their attention, and they moved to Church Hill for what was to prove a long and happy last stage in their lives. They particularly enjoyed the extensive views to both front and back. They came to know the Island intimately, first as keen walkers and also as motorists who were additionally willing to leave their car to explore in all seasons. Above all, Godshill - both place and people -- meant a great deal to them, including the Sunshine Club which they ran for 11 years, and All Saints Church. JVJ was also for a period on the list as Local Preacher on the Methodist Circuit.

Quietly, indeed privately, he pursued an interest in the history of the Island, and in particular of the Church, Village and Parish of Godshill. On his death, among his belongings were six ring-files containing about 450 pages of closely typed material on local history, of which most people had been previously permitted to see only the covers of the files. It is from those pages that the contents of this book are drawn.

EDITORIAL NOTE

JVJ's style of writing shows several characteristics which it did not seem appropriate to retain. His lifetime as a School-teacher had shown him the value of repetition in penetrating the memory of young lads. It also led him to personalise events, for example into the reign of each sovereign, and then to attribute acts of government to the monarch personally. His prose writing style bore traces of the poet that is in every Welshman, and the Editor has reluctantly decided to use a more prosaic style in this published work. A handicap that JVJ was subject to was that he had only a typewriter without electronic memory. This is an unforgiving method by comparison with the 'word-processing' facility so readily available today. The reader is also asked to remember that JVJ did not live on the Island until he was in his sixties, and his work continued into his eighties.

It is good advice to anyone starting to study the local history of a place to have recourse first to printed material, and this seems to have been the process followed by JVJ. This book cannot lay claim to contain a work of original scholarship, and in particular is almost completely bereft of reference to sources, and thus acknowledgment of such sources. This absence results from those of JVJ's working notes as have been preserved containing none, except for a short Bibliography reproduced below. A general apology is thus included at this point for any source left unacknowledged.

Finally, the reader is asked to remember two difficulties that JVJ's first Editor has had to labour under: he has never himself lived on the Island, and has not been able (or willing to devote the time) to check sources or even identify errors. We hope that the two local editors have managed this!

Contents

(References to present monetary value:
'the present' should be taken to mean the 1980s
when much of the original was written)

PREFACE

SOME FACTS from the DOMESDAY BOOK

From early centuries we often receive legends. For example a Tourist Guide may refer to the tenacious belief that the site chosen for the first Christian church was on level ground ('Devil's Acre') a mile to the south. It continues that when work started on the building, the materials were miraculously moved during the night to the present site. After three such experiences, the builders were convinced that the Almighty had chosen the Knoll for his Church, and they complied with his will. The Anglo-Saxon building was on the present Church site on 'God's Hill', (which was highly likely to have been previously a site of pagan worship, thus originally named 'Gods' Hill').

For facts, we must turn to the famous 'book', which contains the results of the survey conducted for William the Conqueror in 1086, twenty years after the dramatic start to his reign. Specific questions were asked in relation to the situation on three occasions:

> before the Conquest under Anglo-Saxon manorial lords;
> immediately after, when they had been replaced by Normans;
> and in 1086, after disputes both within the new landholding class,
>   and between secular and church landlords.

Note the final words in the preamble. This was a survey for purposes of taxation.

"Here follows the inquiry concerning lands which the King's barons made according to the oaths of the sheriff of the county and of all the barons and their Frenchmen, and of the whole hundred court - the priest, the reeve, and six villagers from each village. They enquired what the manor was called; who held it in 1066; who holds it now; how many hides there are; how many ploughteams in demesne and how many belonging to the men; how many villagers; how many cottagers; how many slaves; how many freemen; how many sokemen; how much woodland; how much meadow; how much pasture; how many mills; how many fisheries; how much has been added to or taken away from the manor; what it was worth and what it is worth now; and how much each freeman and sokeman had and has. All this was recorded thrice: as it was in 1066, when King William granted the manor, and now.

And it was also noted whether more could be taken from the manor than is now being taken."

One question was about the value of each estate, and it is to this that we restrict this preface. Actual figures are given here, not to show value in isolation, for inflation renders that impossible, but to indicate the *relative* worth of the estates.

	in 1066	in 1086
Sandford with Week	£20	£20 (£26 + l00d)
Roud	£9 (later £8)	£7 10s.
Stenbury	£6	£6
Bathingboume	£4	£4
Lessland	20s.	20s.
Appleford (North)	20s.	10s.
Appleford (Great)	17s.	18s.
Appleford (Upper)	10s.	10s.
Bagwich	5s.	3s.

ONE
EARLY MEDIEVAL GODSHILL

A site of worship set on a knoll, gave its name to the little hamlet clustered around it, and thus to the man, William de Godeshylla, who was the first recorded priest there. The thatched Anglo-Saxon church standing on this prominent site was soon replaced by a small stone one, for the Normans built in stone to signify strength, and at Godshill they believed the site to be God-given. Of the Norman structure very little survives (such as a detached capital discovered in the Tower, and scraps of re-used stone).

William Fitz-Osbern, kinsman of the Conqueror, had been given absolute power under the Crown as overlord of the Island. Anglo-Saxon thanes were ousted and replaced by his Norman knights. The family of de Aula was rewarded with the manor of Stenbury. De Roucley was given what became Rookley Manor. Fitz-azors was granted Appleford and Roud manors. Two Norman monastic houses (Lyra and Montesbourg) founded by Fitz-Osbern and under his patronage were granted feudal Lordship of the Manors of Godshill and Appuldurcombe respectively. To Lyra he also gave Godshill and five other churches on the Island. Fitz-Osbern died in battle on the continent in 1070.

A manor was an economic unit. The scene across that part of the Island was of a series of manors, independent of each other and at first with uncultivated land between. The area later covered by the village of Godshill was little different, save for the important presence of the Church on the Knoll. This served all the manors in the extensive parish of Godshill, the names of most of which have survived to the present day. Smaller Lords with a single Manor were likely to be resident, and owed certain duties to at least one overlord and then to the King, the head of the feudal pyramid. The simple Manor house would be surrounded by the humbler dwellings of freemen, villeins and serfs all linked in various ways economically to their lord.

From 1066 to 1295 the Island was troubled by only minor invasion from abroad, but warlike incursions by marauding bands were a fact of life: men bent on plunder and not stopping short of murder. The first level of protection was that afforded by the manor itself, but a further resort was the stone church building, and records indicate that such bands did assail the Church at Godshill. To prepare the Island's defences, King Edward I purchased the Lordship of the Island and appointed three Wardens

A small Benedictine Priory had been founded at Appuldurcombe in the parish of Godshill as daughter house or cell to Montesbourg - see section 3. The Prior was supported by two or three Monks and a household of lay brothers, mostly Norman-French. Together with a larger Priory at Carisbrooke it was under obedience to the fully established house in Normandy. At Appuldurcombe the Prior was responsible for managing the surrounding estate and collecting its dues and tithes.

William the Priest and his successor from 1160 Simon of Godshill were nominated ultimately by the Norman monastery of Lyra who owned Godshill Church. They continued to combat the ignorance and pre-Christian practice undoubtedly still present there. The earlier struggle to convert the Island to Christianity had never been complete, and it readily relapsed.

The influence of the monks was not totally benign, for they were from the same foreign land as those who lorded it over the native islanders and moreover extracted no little income from them. The local origin and foreign destination of produce and funds were the raw material of conflict with the islanders. The people of the parish were resentful and bitter towards the aliens. In Godshill one can only suppose that antipathy between village and Priory increased. In any event, those native to the Island were never likely to be well-disposed to the men originating south of the Channel while the land was subjected to sporadic attacks by bands of sailors and soldiers from the continent as was the case at that time. A confusing aspect for us is that Plantagenet Kings of England had lands across the Channel and were at home there. Henry II was born, frequently lived and was buried not in the English part of his Kingdom but in what is today called France.

A visible symbol of division between the monks and the native islanders came with the extension of Godshill church. On the south side of the existing building was erected a matching range of chancel and nave, exclusively for the Prior, monks, lay brothers and tenants from Appuldurcombe. Each side was entered by its own door, and there were in effect two churches side by side. The south side was the more comfortable. In later re-building the division remained, emphasised by a parclose.[1]

After Simon, there is no record of another priest in the parish for about a century. It was not unusual for Church livings to be held in suspense for purely selfish financial reasons, the net income being swollen by the reduction in expenditure.

---

[1] ecclesiastical screen

Underlying this turbulence was an intense struggle for dominance between the authorities. An example of the English Crown attempting to increase its control was the Act of Mortmain 1279. This was designed to prevent further land falling into the 'dead hand' (mort main) of a Corporation such as the Church. On the Island it was bitterly opposed by the Priors of Appuldurcombe and Carisbrooke. At the same period, however, there were proven cases of foreign monks having grossly misused funds.

From 1312 the incumbent at Godshill was no longer Rector but Vicar (see section 8). The timing of this change may also be linked with the foregoing difficulties.

There were complex business arrangements made in respect of tithes. Godshill was an example of a geographically large parish whose tithes were apportioned.

Albin confirms that in 1305 the Abbot of Lyra in Normandy was receiving both the great and small tithes from the Godshill Tythings of Week, Appuldurcombe and Godshill Manor, and also from William de Heyno of Stenbury Manor. He states that the Abbot of Quarr received the tithes from John Lisle of Roud Manor, and. some went to the Rector of St Lawrence and some to the Rector of Gatcombe. De Welford departed owing a debt for tithe!

Incidentally, soon after this time, both the lords of Stenbury Manor and the family of Lisle were granted the necessary licences for chapels, presumably chantries. William de Heyno renounced the claim he had made to the Godshill advowson, which was restored and confirmed to the Abbey of Lyra.

In the middle of the 14th century, Edward III was locked in hostilities with the French, and was claiming the throne there. Most of the military and naval action was away from English shores, but the French fleet did make opportunist raids on the Isle of Wight. Attempts were made to strengthen the defences. Godshill, as did other parishes, sent one bowman to serve with the Island Militia which was trained as a defensive force. Archery was a sport long since encouraged in readiness for such a situation. The leader of the Militia was John Hackett of Wolverton Manor, a descendent of whom was later buried in Godshill Church (though the tomb has not survived).

A local man prominent in the Island Militia was Peter de Heyno, Lord of the Manor of Stenbury. Legend has it that he brought a severely wounded French Officer to the churchyard at Godshill, but there his adversary died and was buried in the stone coffin that remains to this day. Be that as it may, there is a factual reminder of the de Heyno family, for one was buried by the path leading to the South Porch. The marauding French were surprised by the military efficiency of the Militia, and suffered at their hands in many a bloody skirmish. The term of derision current among the English was 'Noddies'. Thus, where one today finds a place on the Island with a name such as Noddy Hill or Cottage, or Nodes Hill, it is highly likely to indicate a success for the Militia in a military encounter as early as the 13th century.

During the 14th century, the control exercised by Bishops within their dioceses was often needed to uphold the material welfare of parish priests. Bishops resisted abuse of absentee control and the putting in of unbeneficed curates, rather than beneficed vicars. In a case at Brading, it was established what the priest should receive in funeral dues and altar oblations, and what produce (listed) might be offered by way of tithes. There is reference to giving service by digging on the vicar's land or by supplying fish. We are so used to a cash economy that such remuneration in kind is surprising to us. At this time, three acres was seen as the minimum area of land for the incumbent, but he was expected to build the parsonage house at his own expense. Nothing is known of such a house in Godshill, and in later times there was no parsonage house.

The vicars of this turbulent time, after Harry de Wellford, were:

Martin de Gastena/Gasterd	1334 - 1335
Nicholas de Wolveley/Wolodeye	1335 - 1336
Thomas de Fretwell	1336 - 1349

The French names should not be assumed to indicate lack of sympathy with native English ways. French was the language that survived in legal and academic use.

On the mainland in mid-century the greatest single cause of social upheaval was the Great Plague. Some 'overners' did manage to escape to the Island, bringing the plague with them, but there is no record of exceptional death in Godshill. Nevertheless, there was great fear and much seeking after divine protection through the Church.

A
BARTON ORATORY

Thomas de Wyntonia (Vicar of Godshill from 1275 to 1284), his curate Jordan de Marisca and a third clergyman in 1282 jointly founded an Oratory. At a hamlet called Barton in Whippingham Parish, about 8 miles north of Godshill, they set up this small independent community as a centre of prayer. Six Chaplains, one of whom was to be Warden, together with a Clerk were to devote their lives to prayer for both the living and the departed. Their Rule was modelled on those of St Augustine, and they were known by abbreviation as 'Austin' Canons, and from their dress as Black Canons. They owed obedience to the Warden, who was answerable to the patron whom they had chosen, the Bishop of Winchester, rather than to a Superior of any other community. In that sense they were independent. Their income was derived from the Manor (now extinct) of Croodman (IoW).

They held their possessions in common, and took full vows after a year's probationary period. Thereafter, a man might not accept a benefice as a parish priest or indeed leave. Their diet was frugal, and their Rule required that each day the meal was to be shared with 13 poor men who were to sit down with them. Meals were taken in silence, with the Clerk giving an edifying reading. The Warden took the head of the table. A set order of seating gave the next place to the Chaplain whose turn it had been to celebrate Mass that morning. Comment on the food served was forbidden.

Over their black habits, a surplice was worn as appropriate. Out of doors, they added a coarse black woollen cloak, and a cap. They were never to walk alone, but always with a fellow Chaplain, leaving the precincts of the Oratory only with permission of the Warden. Each year on All Saints Day they were provided with a new habit, but as none were permitted more than two, one would be given away at the Gate to beggars.

The routine of each day was set by the Rule. They rose before day-break in winter, and at sun-rise in summer. They were to be diligent in reading the scriptures and in saying prayers. One of their number (the Precentor) wrote the following week's programme of Masses and duties on a tablet which was displayed after dinner. As a constant reminder, the whole text of the Rule was read aloud to the community at least once a month, with severe punishment for breach.

Sad to relate, during the 14th century, lax conduct of the Canons frequently needed to be called to the attention of the Diocesan authorities. The accusations included unspecified breach of vows, neglect of the Rule and improper use of funds. Complaints came to a climax in the time of Bishop William of Wykeham (1367-1404) and he appointed a Commission to enquire into the Wardenship of William Love and the affairs of the Oratory. Love was found guilty of misappropriation of funds, neglect of the fabric of the building and lack of supervision of the conduct of the Oratory in general. The house was in a ruinous condition and the Bishop ordered it to be repaired. Within a few years however, in 1439, the house was surrendered into the hands of the Bishop and the lands granted by him to Winchester College.

No link with Godshill Church remained.

TWO
LATER MIDDLE AGES and EARLY TUDORS

French invaders penetrated to Godshill in the 1350s, and again attacked the Island in the 1370s. 1377 is doubly memorable as the year that Edward III died, and the year of the Poll Tax. In order to replenish the Exchequer after the many years of war, for the first time in England this personal tax was introduced.

Vicars:
John Kynge	1349 -1382
William Ashrugge	1383 - 1393
John Kelseye	1393 - 1403.

The mid 14th century is the period of a re-building of All Saints in the late (transitional) Decorated style. Only part of this work is now visible, such as the tracery of the two east windows, one reticulated and one with branch tracery.

The parish of Godshill at that period was of considerable size, the boundaries dating back to Anglo-Saxon times. The parish extended to the south-east sea-coast, giving access not only for obvious purposes but providing also a share in salvage of wrecks and flotsam and jetsam. The incumbent had responsibilities over this wide area, and a 'monopoly' of certain rights of which one was the place and fees of burial. For those transporting the body of the deceased, the substantial distance from the edges of the parish represented an onerous solemn duty.

The vicars of Godshill are likely to have dressed in long black robes of rough quality with cowls, and to have been celibate, constantly watched over by those in authority in the monastic houses on the Island. The collection of tithes was a constant anxiety and there is record of a dispute with the tithepayer of Rew Farm. At this time, accusations were also made against the Priors of both Appuldurcombe and Carisbrooke of partiality towards the French, whose bands of adventurers continued to trouble the Island. Edward III had instructed the Bishop of Winchester to cause the expulsion of such sympathisers, and a Prior and two monks did indeed leave.

A dispute within the Church led to the punishment of a Prior and five incumbents on the Island, although the Vicar of Godshill was not one. This resulted from papal action against absenteeism, the practice of the legal incumbent appointing a priest as deputy at a low wage and himself either living at ease elsewhere or taking an additional post ('plurality'). When the Bishop of Winchester with Papal support dismissed the Rector of Freshwater, strong reaction from Island clergy led to excommunication.

The discipline of the Island defence notable in the reign of Edward III was relaxed under his grandson and successor, and this was a terrible time for local residents, as John Stow the later historian was to record. 'The French took that invincible island more by craft than force', and he blamed the Watch for failing in their duty. Some Islanders fled to the mainland, risking forfeit of their lands and possessions to the Crown. Most retreated with what possessions they could carry to Carisbrooke Castle. Parts of the Island were put to the torch by the French.

Animals were herded away in readiness for shipping across the Channel. Godshill would not have escaped, though evidence is sparse. The invaders laid siege to Carisbrooke Castle, but failed to capture it. They did however exact a promise of tribute of 1,000 marks as the price of leaving without further destruction of homes, and were permitted to return unmolested to their ships. When they returned the next year, both the Watch and the Militia were better prepared.

On another occasion in 1399, a large fleet of French Men-of-War anchored off the east of the Island. The Officer of the Fleet claimed that the King and his Queen were held hostage, and demanded a ransom. However, the Captain of the Island was better informed than the French had supposed, for the news of the death of the King had already reached him, and he knew too that his Queen had returned to her native France. He challenged the French force to disembark, offering them six hours to prepare and refresh themselves, before engaging in pitched battle with the Militia. The challenge was not accepted and the French set sail and retired from the scene.

Foreign aggression continued from Spaniards as well as French. In 1418, a body of French privateering adventurers landed on the Isle, boasting that they intended to celebrate Christmas there. About a thousand began combing the land for cattle, sheep and other livestock, which they herded towards their ships anchored off the south coast. A well organised Militia attack inflicted casualties and drove the remainder off the island without their plunder.

There were several occasions of conflict between the Crown and alien Priories. In 1414, the earlier expulsion of French monks was taken a step further with Crown action to close the alien Priories at Appuldurcombe and Carisbrooke. Thus came to an end the sense so prevalent among native landowners that the beneficiaries of their tithes were foreign monastic houses and moreover fellow countrymen of those who attacked the Island. Two religious houses received royal grants of the rights that were confiscated. The Minoresses had a Convent just outside London to the east, working among the destitute of the city in association with Franciscan Friars. Their prize was the Appuldurcombe Estate, with renewed grant later in the 15th century.

The community that received both Godshill Manor and Godshill Church was the 'royal' Carthusian house at Sheen west of London. They retained it until the Dissolution. The monks of Sheen began to design and reconstruct almost the whole of All Saints Church for the third and last time, in the Perpendicular style. Niches in the columns on the central axis of the Church still reveal today the position of the parclose that was removed to re-unite the two halves of the church. Cardinal Henry Beaufort's Book setting out the value of Church livings shows Godshill as yielding the highest income of all the parishes on the Island. The priests having charge of the Church through this century did not of course receive the whole income. They were:

Roger Tydeman	1403 - 1440
Richard Mackeyt	1440 - 1477
Richard Mackeyt his son	1477 - 1493
Henry Seygoure	1493 - 1509

Clerical celibacy was a firm policy in the Church of Rome. This did not however prevent the son of Mackeyt from following his father in 1477. A clerical marriage was not void unless challenged, and there are many known cases, until at the Reformation the English Church broke from the Roman regulation. (On the Isle of Wight, however, a married priest was for many years regarded by the gentry as of lower social status.)

The second half of the 15th century was a more peaceful period, since the power struggle known as the Wars of the Roses had little effect on the Island. For a period it was without its Crown - appointed Lord, but in due course, King Henry VII appointed Sir Edward Woodville to succeed his brother.

Sir Edward Woodville was the enthusiastic supporter of the Duke of Brittany who was locked in conflict with King Charles VIII of France. When Henry VII declined to take military action in support of Brittany, Sir Edward in 1488 roused the men of the Island to take up arms against the King of France. A force was quickly raised of 40 Gentlemen and Officers and 400 volunteers. Dressed in white uniform-coat with red crosses, they gathered at St Helens (IoW) and embarked in four ships. They were supported by the Island people, who saw this venture as a manly response to the marauding bands of French privateers at whose hands they had suffered in the past. Joining with 1,500 men of the Duke of Brittany similarly attired, they were soon confronted by a larger force at St Aubens in Brittany, and were decisively defeated.

It is said that only one Isle of Wight man survived the slaughter, a boy who was permitted to return to break the dreadful news to the Islanders. Royal displeasure was a factor in the cessation of royal appointments to Lordship of the Isle. Moreover, the death of such a high proportion of the able-bodied men of the community may help to explain an Act of Parliament. No-one was to possess property exceeding in annual value 10 marks, in the belief that this would restore the male population of the Isle of Wight. The Crown was also concerned to check the power of laymen far from the Court.

An inventory of property on the island ordered by the King in 1507 (including Church patronage) shows that there was no Crown property in the parish of Godshill.

From the incumbency of the Godshill Vicar Thomas Bayly (1509 - 1527) a surviving document records a complaint by the congregation of the Chapel of St Rhadegund and St Mary's, the only 'church' at Whitwell. This was not a simple issue, because of its long history. In the 12th century, the notable family Estur of Gatcombe had built a Chantry dedicated to St. Rhadegund in the village of Whitwell (the chancel of the present church). Whitwell, 3 miles south of Godshill village, was then within Godshill parish. In the 15th century there was a Chapel of Ease, St Mary's, for which the Vicar of Godshill was responsible. This dual spiritual responsibility was housed in a single building, and latterly, income was shared. The Vicar of Godshill officiated. The Rector of Gatcombe should have assisted him but the distance made this inconvenient and he preferred to make an annual payment of 4 nobles (£1.6s.8d) on the basis of the Vicar of Godshill performing the whole duty.

For many years this joint arrangement seems to have worked satisfactorily, but in 1515 the residents of Whitwell did make complaint, possibly a fiction to bring their status inexorably to the attention of the authorities. They alleged that that their sacred treasures had been misappropriated by Master Bayly and the Rector of Gatcombe. The Bishop of Winchester found in favour of the people and ordered restoration of these disputed items. The opportunity was taken by the Bishop to respond to what was perhaps the basic issue, reminding both sides to the dispute of their obligations: the clerics to provide services and care for the people, and the people to maintain their respective parts of the shared building.   In course of time, Whitwell did receive a Royal Grant creating it a separate parish (see section 8).

The south transept of Godshill Church had probably already been a Chantry Chapel of the Fitz-Azors and the Hacketts.   William Hackett had been interred in the church in the reign of Henry VII. As is seen in Section 7, Sir John Leigh had come to Appuldurcombe by marriage to a Hackett, and this may account for his being licensed in 1520 to re-endow it as a Chantry Chapel for his family. Sir John Leigh died in 1522, and Lady Agnes in 1525, and their monument is in the church where they too were buried.   Their daughter married Sir James Worsley, and in 1527 the Abbess of the Minoress house Without Aldgate leased Appuldurcombe to him as a private residence, together with the tithes of Godshill.

The Vicars of Godshill through this time of religious turmoil and declaration of independence from Rome were:
    Thomas Bradshaw   1527 - 1538
    Robert Thorpe   1538 - 1543

Most of the changes made in the six-year reign of Edward VI were to be reversed when Mary came to the throne, and changed again five years later on her death. The Vicar, George Cotes, was to retain his benefice for 24 years through the religiously diverse reigns of four monarchs.

One of the results of the Dissolution of the Monasteries was the closure of a source of charitable provision for the poor. This is dealt with in section D. Another result was that valuable assets came into the hands of the Crown. These included not only the monastic sites themselves but also their portfolios of investments and sources of influence including advowsons. These were mostly disposed of by the Crown, either by sale or as gift to those whose loyalty the King wished to secure.

In 1538 Sir Thomas Wriothesley, later Earl of Southampton, a favoured ambassador for Henry VIII, unsuccessfully applied for the advowson and glebeland of Godshill. These rights were in fact granted to a Southampton businessman named George Mill, but on the change of religious & political rule the rights were forfeit back to the Crown. Queen Mary bestowed them on her (Catholic) Bishop of Winchester.

Before the end of the reign of Henry VIII the Island was to suffer further incursions of hostile forces, which must have seemed to the residents of Godshill parish of greater immediacy than who would decide upon the identity of the next vicar.

B
MANOR COURT and CHANGING SOCIETY

A successful military defence against French marauders was likely to be followed by a period of peace. The people of Godshill, as elsewhere on the Island, could concentrate on farming their rich arable soil and minding their livestock. On each manor, justice and order was in theory secure through the Manorial Court, and courts dealt with many aspects of life that we would consider not judicial but administrative.

14th century court records have survived of Skotland Manor at the west end of the parish. The old 'Scotland House' was demolished in 1911, but the site continued to carry the name with the building of a new dwelling.

Here we meet the Steward or Seneschal who presided on behalf of the Lord, the Reeve who was general Estate Manager, and the Hayward who had more immediate oversight of the open-field husbandry and the use of common lands. Fines were imposed on offenders, not only in the sense of minor criminal activity but simply for practices which were troublesome to the Lord of the Manor, or made unacceptably difficult the close working relationships of his people. Medieval living required strict discipline over such matters as boundaries, water-supply and the disposal of human waste. Tine was also the word for payment for permission from the Lord to do or escape doing something which the Lord by custom was entitled to control. It was a source of income for the feudal superior, and an assertion of his lordship. Land transactions in particular had to be approved and recorded by the Steward, a fee charged, and the new holder had importantly to acknowledge the seigneurial rights. The word 'surrender' conveys the hierarchical tone which would remain the essence of copyhold relationships well into the 20th century.

The Royal courts were far away, expensive and to be avoided by all but the high status litigant. The Consistory courts, for example at Winchester, dealt with moral matters and anything to do with death and inheritance. Between them and the manorial courts was the Island 'Knighten' Court, the forerunner of the Magistrates' Court.

***

The latter part of the 14th century was a time of substantial social change, accelerated across the country by the ravages of the Black Death. Serfs were either granted their freedom or unilaterally took it. Some never again had land to cultivate which could in any sense be called their own. Others became husbandmen with independence of the manorial lord. Land was cleared and brought under cultivation or made available for grazing. The acute demand for labour meant that the personal link of serfdom was being replaced by wages to landless and thus mobile labourers, but freedom of contract soon operated against those very labourers who had at first welcomed it.

The village of Godshill grew.

THREE
THE APPULDURCOMBE ESTATE - 1066 to 1603

In the valley between Stenbury Down and Wroxall Down, narrow at the south, but widening as the little river flows northwards, lies the heart of the historic estate of Appuldurcombe. The name derives not from orchards but from three geographical words meaning 'bottom of a watered little valley'. Most of the Appuldurcombe estate was within the large parish of Godshill, and at its height included several manors.

After Henry I granted Lordship of the Isle to Richard de Redvers early in the 12th century, he in turn conferred many of the rights and profits of the Estate at Appuldurcombe on the Abbot of Montesbourg. This was a Benedictine monastic house in Normandy, the land from which his family had come. This led to the creation of a small cell or daughter Priory in the Appuldurcombe valley, with a Prior and two monks. With serf labour and the help of lay brothers, they constructed the monastic buildings, and thereafter managed the estate and collected its produce, not only from Appuldurcombe but also from Sandford & Week. (The de Redvers family retained the Lordship of the Island until 1283, when on there failing to be a male heir, it passed to a sister: Isabella de Fortibus.)

The monks of this Priory with their lay brothers had as their church the southern part of All Saints Church. Until the mid 14th century the Priory was financially prosperous, but over the centuries its foreign origin became not only a source of bitterness among the indigenous islanders, but also a national concern. The English Crown was at war with parts of France, and the Island was in the front line. By Royal Order in 1340 the Prior and two monks were removed to Hyde Abbey near Winchester during the war.

The Priory was under feudal obligation like any lay lord in time of war to furnish 2 knights, 2 archers and certain defined military equipment. An Inventory of equipment surviving from that time shows readiness to fulfil this service: a suit of armour with accoutrements, 2 haketons (padded tunics), 2 metal-bound coffers, 2 pairs of gisarmes (halberds), 2 audersons (hauberks to protect neck & shoulders), 2 pairs of musttelers, (knee caps) and 2 broken capitalia (headgear).

In addition, the substantial peacetime wealth was listed: 80 quarters of wheat, 20 quarters of dredge (mixed) corn, 2 oxen, 3 cows and a bull with 2 bullocks & 9 calves, 2 horses, 131 sheep and 248 ewes with 4 rams & 160 lambs, 6 sows & 76 piglets, 80 hens, 4 weys of cheese (a wey being potentially 3 cwt) and 4 x 41.28 bushels (5 stones) of wool.

Some years later, Appuldurcombe Priory Estate was annexed by the Crown, and then granted to a poor English house of the Order of St Clare: the Abbey of Minoresses Without Aldgate, London, where the sisters worked among the sick and destitute. (Minoresses were nuns associated with the Franciscan Friars). They appear to have treated it as investment property. Further Royal Grants in the 15th century gave that house fuller ownership of the Appuldurcombe estate, and about 1485 a lease of the Priory buildings and farm was created in favour of an Island lay resident named Fry. On his death shortly afterwards, his widow Agnes married Sir John Leigh. In 1498, Sir John Leigh took a further lease of the Priors' residence, and the Leighs were then in possession of a desirable estate to which they moved, and work began to convert the residence to a Tudor Manor House. An accumulation of property was not normally permitted by the Crown, but in this instance a Royal Dispensation was sealed in 1505. This enabled Sir John Leigh, his wife Agnes and her daughter Joan Fry to hold "the Manor or Priory of Appuldurcombe" in addition to the Priory of Carisbrooke and other lands on the Island already owned.

The Leighs had a daughter named Anne. Sir John Leigh died in 1522, and his widow three years later. They were buried in All Saints Church Godshill, 'facing the altar where the priest normally commences his "confiteor" in front of the lowest step'. Their monument with alabaster figures, situated between the two chancels, has been described by the diarist Oglander "as the fairest tomb in our Island". Their daughter Anne inherited Sir John Leigh's estate.

About 1516, two brothers Giles and James Worsley had moved from the north of England to the Isle of Wight. The family name links with the estate of Worsley in Lancashire, but in fact they traced their lineage back to the Conquest. James had earlier been a pageboy at Court, and through this connection a boyhood friend of Henry who was to succeed his father as Henry VIII in 1509. Through Henry James Worsley was given all the offices giving control on the Island: Coroner, Sheriff, Constable of Carisbrooke Castle (when it should fall vacant) and from 1511 military Captaincy of the Isle of Wight. Moreover, for services at 'the Field of the Cloth of Gold' in 1520, he was knighted.

Sir James married the Appuldurcombe heiress Anne Leigh, and they obtained a further extension by lease of 35 years, from the Abbess at Aldgate, thus giving greater security at Appuldurcombe.   Sir James Worsley made generous charitable grants to the Abbey towards the repair and extension of the hospice, and also made loans since the house was "in great need and necessities". The suppression of that house at the general Dissolution did not affect the rights of Sir James at Appuldurcombe as his lease was a right to property, but the Crown became his landlord. This was a time of dispersal of great riches from the dissolved religious houses, administered through the Court of Augmentation, and Sir James was among those who benefited. He was politically the most powerful man on the Island, and Appuldurcombe Manor House correspondingly prominent, worthy to receive a royal visit, but that came to his successor.

Sir James Worsley died in 1538, to be succeeded by his son Richard. He had bequeathed to the King his best gold chain and his largest gold standing cup, and to Thomas Cromwell, dispenser of so many royal favours, another such cup. To Godshill Church he bequeathed some rich vestments, and to the Chantry Grammar School an annual sum of £11 with a pension to the retiring Master one John Griffin MA.

Lady Anne Worsley was an adherent to the older ways of Rome, and made periodic pilgrimages to holy shrines on the Continent. She had been in dispute with the Vicar who had Protestant sympathies, but she continued her late husband's patronage of the School at Chantry House. It was she who obtained licence during the reign of Edward VI to use Chantry funds to re-establish the Grammar School in the village. She lived through the Protestant period and through most of the reign of the Catholic Queen Mary. On her death 19 years after him, Lady Anne was buried with her husband, and the colourful monument to them both is prominent on the north wall of All Saints Church.

Sir Richard Worsley became Captain of the Wight after his father, and it was when inspecting the military defences that King Henry VIII is reliably recorded as being entertained at Appuldurcombe with his chief Minister Thomas Cromwell, Earl of Essex. It has been suggested that Essex Cottage in Godshill was so named in memory of that Minister. Several times Sir Richard Worsley was called upon to exercise leadership in military matters, for this was a time of sporadic attacks by both French and Spanish marauding bands. One of the new defences was called Worsley Tower in his honour. One source of funds for the defences was from the sale of 'popish' Church property including from Godshill, and Sir Richard was supervising Commissioner (see section 4).

Sir Richard had a reputation as a man of great personal quality and learning, and (unlike his Mother) his sympathies were with the new ways in religion. He and his wife, a young heiress from Somerset named Ursula St Barbe, had two sons, John and George. When King Edward died in 1553, Sir Richard had been established at Appuldurcombe for fifteen years, but he was to be an early victim of the changes introduced by the Catholic Queen Mary. He was dismissed from his public posts of Captain of the Isle of Wight and as Justice of the Peace, and forced to live quietly as a country gentleman at his seat for the five years of the reign. Under Elizabeth the new Queen, however, he returned to public life as Member of Parliament for Newport (IoW) and was reinstated in his earlier posts. Sir Richard Worsley died in 1565, having contracted smallpox then prevalent in London where he was fulfilling his public duties. His Will contained bequests of £10 to the Vicar of Godshill, £5 to the Master of the Grammar School Anthony Byrteswell, and £10 to the priest who preached at his funeral.

In the normal course he would have been succeeded by one of his two sons when of age, but a tragic accident with gunpowder took the lives of both boys. This happened in the Porter's Lodge at Appuldurcombe, which was also their schoolroom. "The servants were drying of powder there against the general muster; a sparke flew into the dish, that sett fire to a barrel which stood by, blew up a side of the gatehouse, killed the two children, and some others, hurt one James Worsley a youth, their kinsman ... that went to schole there with them, who has often told me this story' (Sir John Oglander).

The young widow Lady Ursula did re-marry, and a man of national repute: Sir Francis Walsingham, the Queen's Secretary of State for Foreign Affairs. He was in effect for 17 years Head of the Secret Service, frustrating the many enemies of the Queen. He was never rich, died in poverty in 1590, and caused Lady Ursula to die in London in poverty also.

Appuldurcombe had passed in 1565 to the younger brother of Sir Richard, John, and he had married Jane of the Island family of Mew/Meux whose home was Kingston Manor. John erected on the south wall of All Saints a monument, with the family arms and chief quarterings and inscription, to his brother and young nephews.

At the Dissolution, the family had bought leases and tithes formerly vested in the local monastic houses. The Worsley History (1781) records that on succeeding his brother, John 'had a long contest with Sir Francis Walsingham, for the chattel estates; but Walsingham prevailing, enjoyed, in right of his wife, the leases of Boucombe, the priory of Carisbrook, the manors of Godshill and Freshwater; which were then of great value.' Ownership of Godshill manor was not acquired by the Worsley family until much later.

Sir Francis Walsingham became guardian to young Thomas, the only son of John and Jane Worsley. In due course Thomas married the daughter of a well - known man of property in Hampshire, distantly related to the royal house of Tudor through the mother of Henry VII. Thomas was moving socially among influential families such as the Nevilles, Wallops, Herberts and Thynnes. Thomas succeeded his father in 1580. Thomas was described at the time as 'being well learned in the arts of education and a man of very good character.' To his wife, the conditions at Appuldurcombe were rustic and unsophisticated. During the reign of Queen Elizabeth the old Priory House was thoroughly 'modernised' to the status of a Tudor Manor House.

Richard, the elder son of Thomas went to Winchester School, where the lad took an active part in school life, but on the hunting field suffered an accident which caused the loss of one eye. When he was 15, his father Thomas died. Richard went on to Magdalene College Oxford, where his classical education was guided by a tutor named Castillion. At age 21, Richard Worsley accompanied his tutor on a perambulation on the mainland, which included a visit to the Lincolnshire seat of Sir Henry Neville. There Richard met a daughter of the house, Mistress Frances Neville, and they were later married, a union that was described as 'fancy prevailing over portion'.

Richard was obliged to swear that he personally was not previously contracted to marry anyone else. This was necessary because his father had entered into a private arrangement earlier creating a conditional betrothal between Richard and Honora, the daughter of John White from Wiltshire, and recorded it in his Will. It was linked with a secured loan which Thomas Worsley had made to White, which it appears was repayable only if the marriage did not take place at the request of White. Honora later married the wealthy Sir Daniel Norton, and this potentially explosive situation ended 'happily and honestly as in the character of Sir Richard'.

In taking up residence at Appuldurcombe with his wife, Richard Worsley banned hawking and hunting on his land, no doubt in reaction against a sport which had cost him the loss of an eye. Through the good offices of Sir Henry Neville, Richard was knighted, and the couple gained a reputation for generous hospitality, 'family happiness, courteousness, artistic disposition and generosity to all their friends and servants'.

C
TUDOR MANOR HOUSE

Appuldurcombe House in the time of the Leighs and the next few generations was 'E' shaped, in the fashion of the times. Although it did not survive, there are many such houses in England today that have retained the Tudor domestic style. The house had a Hall, two Chambers (Great and Little) and six principal bedrooms. These were named: Paradise, the Broad, Sir John's, The Porch, Mr Richard Worsley's and My Lady's Chamber. Two smaller bedrooms were for the children. There was a Chapel, and three secondary chambers named The Maidens, The Green and Mrs Brenshott's.

There were three small bedrooms for the main domestic servants plus two others for the Bailiff and the married farm servant who lived in. There were two kitchens, a wet Larder, a dry Larder, a brewhouse, a malthouse, a stillatory (presumably for preparation of drink) and a dairy. All these were in the main building. Outside were large stables with two bedrooms for permanent ostlers, and the horses kept would have served various purposes for riding, hunting, carriage work, and a variety of farm tasks. Oxen too were kept for draught work on the farm. Up on the hillside was an ice-house. The gardens were laid out in the fashion of the day and included a bowling green.

By the time of Sir John Leigh, it was usual for the earlier open shelves or boards to be enclosed, and there would be a great Livery Cupboard to keep the food and requisites for the use of the staff, and a Court Cupboard for the dry goods of the Master and Mistress of the house. Sideboards were coming into fashion. Chairs were few, and stools and chests were used for seating. The main table would be of oak and very solid, or cumbersome - according to one's viewpoint. To modern eyes the rooms would look bare but sturdy. There would be no glass mirrors, still a great delicacy. Any fabric would not be on the floor as carpet, but hung on the walls or spread over the table. Rushes would cover the floor, either strewed or loosely plaited.

A Dutch visitor to England wrote: 'the neat cleanliness, the exquisite finesse, the pleasaunte and delightful furniture in every poynte for household, wonderfully rejoiced me, their chambers and their parlours, strawed over with sweet herbs refreshed me; their nosegays finely intermingled with sundry sorte of fragrante flowres in their bedchambers and privy rooms, with comfortable smell, cheered me up and entirely delighted my senses.'

The lady of the house would need to be ready to entertain guests at any time. Barrels of fish would be salted down, and salted meat kept cold. In the storeroom would be pepper, nutmeg, cloves, ginger, figs, dates, raisins, almonds, honey, saffron, hops, oil, vinegar, salt, cinnamon and other flavourings. Roasting was effected on the spit in the kitchen, and there was probably a baking oven at the side of the fireplace. Large quantities of liquid refreshment would be kept in suitable conditions: wines, strong beer, stale ale, mead, cider and perry.

Entertainment for guests in the Great Hall would feature both singing and playing on instruments at least recognisable today, for both accomplishments were part of culture from the Royal Court to the Tudor Manor House.

FOUR
POST - REFORMATION

That radical shift in policy in the 1530s we call the English Reformation had a great variety of results on the Island. In the last year of the old reign and on the accession of young Edward VI in 1547, the outward furnishings of the Catholic way of worship were being removed from Island churches, as throughout the land. The most saleable items were of silver and high quality fabrics. What was specific to the Island was urgent need for funds to pay for increased defence. Sir Richard Worsley as Captain of the Island had been commissioned by the Crown to oversee the sale of Church plate for that purpose, paying proceeds into the Exchequer. In effect the Crown was confiscating valuables under pretext of their religious associations, but was at least using the proceeds on the Island. The Order of 1555 was for a general visitation of churches, but this was after the process had begun. One or two chalices of silver were to be left, with linen for the communion table and surplices. Linen, copes and altar cloths were to be sold and the proceeds given to the poor. All the rest was to be brought in to the Treasurer of the Royal Household. In Godshill a careful record was kept.

Items sold in the old King's reign
    2 challises, 1 sensor of silver weighing 35 ozs   £ 7. 0.0

Items sold in the young King's reign
    1 sensor, a ship, 2 images of silver
    weighing 33 ozs & 90 ozs   £10.9.4
    1 vestment and other implements   £2.3.4
    2 crewets, 1 challis, 2 candlesticks, 1 pyx,)
    silver weighing 4 carat _ oz)   £23 .7.7
    A cross, a pax with a projecting handle bearing a
    representation of the crucifixion weight 57 ozs   £11 .2.4

**Parcels remaining in the custody and charge
of Thomas Kingswill and Robert Bory at this present time**
First, one challes of silver gilte weighing 22ozs 3 quarters
Item, one Cope of red velvet and one vestment bordered with
imagery embroidered with flowers
Item, one cope vestment Deacon and sub-deacon
with damask border & imagery of embroidered flowers and angels
Item, one cope vestment deacon and sub-deacon
Red damask plain border with blue damask
Item, One cope of black damask wosted
Item, One cope of silver dornex
Item, one old blue vestment of satin of breges
Item, cross cloth of red sarsonet

**More remaining in the custody and charge
of Thomas Kingswill and Robert Bory as afore said**
Item, outer clothes
Item, towels
Item, surplices
Item, Hanging in the steeple 4 bells and one little bell
        Hanging in the Church and called the sanctus bell
Item, In the church stock 2 cows and in the said stock 100 sheep
Item, 2 candlesticks of silver

Parcels sold by the Church Parish and churchmen
Item, 2 crewets, one challis and one pyx wighing 10 ozs sold for £1.5.2 by the
hands of John Sander and Christopher Perkins churchwardens by resolution
consent and appointment of the parish as reported in the Church book.
Item, a Cross and a Paxe of silver weighing 46 ozs and sold for 4s.10d per oz sold
by the hands of Christopher Perkins and Thomas Kingswill Churchwardens by
resolution of the parish as recorded in the church book.
Item, 2 challis, one sensor of silver sold by the hands of Robert Morris and John
Coles church wardens by resolution of the Parish but its weight or value was not
recorded in the Church Book and not in their memory

More sold by the parish and church as affore said
Item, one sensor, a ship of silver and 2 images of a cross sold by the hands of
Henry Chestull and John Settforde, Churchwardens appointed by the parish which
is not recorded in the church book nor in their memory.
Item, a cope, a vestment of blue velvet for outside wear, a cope of black satin of
breges to cortens of blue sarsnet the borders of a cope for a deacon and sub-
deacon with imagery embroidery sold by the hands of Christopher Parkins and
Thomas Kingswill church Wardens as recorded in their Church Book.

***

The actions against the faith of the Pope in Rome had other results, for France
was fiercely Roman Catholic, and war against England took on a holy character.
In 1545 a French fleet launched an attack on the Isle of Wight that was designed
to lead to its occupation. This was the occasion of the disastrous capsize and

from the Exchequer via "the Archdeacon of Winton Abbey (Winchester Cathedral) for the Parsons of Godshill and Carisbrooke", presumably because they were by then Crown advowsons.

Mindful that the Incumbent was the leader of his community, those issuing Instructions instructed the Captain to ensure that all parish clergy were in residence in their parishes. Perhaps the chief importance of the incumbent as civil leader of the community was his influence upon the discipline and morale of the people. Godshill Church porch and the Cross in the Churchyard nearby were natural places of assembly. Public notices were posted in the Porch, built early that century, and the Vicar would at service explain them, for many could not read.

In 1567 Godshill had a new Vicar, Henry Hay, who succeeded George Coles, incumbent for 24 years through changing situations. In 1573, his place was taken by William Beale, and after 4 more years by Thomas Gravel (who was to remain in post for 24 years). It should not be supposed that the last forty years of the century were calm in religious matters. There was a growing desire on the part of many to go further than 'the middle way' which Queen Elizabeth was steering between the extremes of the previous two reigns. Within the parish of Godshill, there were groups of Christians particularly at Rookley, Roud and Bagwich who were keen to root out all vestiges of the old faith.

Sir Richard Worsley died in 1565 and the new Captain of the Island was a Devon man: Sir Edward Horsey. A genial seaman, his reputation was of ruthless treatment of the enemy, but his desire for popularity with the Island gentry was allied with a casual approach to maintaining defensive readiness. He preferred to live at Haseley Manor near Arreton rather than the official residence at Carisbrooke Castle. He loved hare coursing and field sports, and it was said that 'a spirit of jollity . . . spread among the people of the Island, helped by the appointment to the captaincy of a typical Elizabethan sea-dog.' But this spirit did not mask the extent of widespread poverty and squalor in the reign of Queen Elizabeth. Along with fear of Spaniards and fear of plague, there was fear of poverty. In her father's time, before the Dissolution of monastic houses, funds sufficient to supplement the provision they made could be raised by voluntary alms given in church. By 1552, the clergy with episcopal encouragement needed to exhort parishioners to greater generosity. Indiscriminate almsgiving was prohibited, as encouraging the idle.

To support the poor of the parish, recourse was then made to a national compulsory levy, and this was repeated. In 1559, two wealthy lay people in the parish contributed 11.63% of the total for the Island, and from this the Vestry were to relieve distress and provide work. The intention was that funds should be used to buy 'a convenient stock of flax, hemp, wool, thread and other materials that would set the poor and destitute to work.' In 1563, by contrast, eighty people in the parish were assessed for taxes to relieve the poor. The Vestry was given greater responsibility under the local Justice of the Peace for civil matters, and the role of Overseer (of the Poor), Constable and Surveyor (of the Highways) gained importance. There was a House of Correction in larger communities; the one in Godshill was not far from the Church.

In 1568 there were two different methods of assessing payment of the levy, one on ownership of land, and the other on goods. The list of the latter for the parish of Godshill is given below, with those most comfortably off given first.

William Legge (£22),
John Wader (£20),
John Sanders (£15),
William Coleman (£14),
William Sanders (£12),
Thomas Tawke, gent (£11),
John Cooke (£11),
John Thomas (£10),
William Game (£10),

Richard Grime (£10),
John Gefferey (£9),
John Kneller (£9),
John Newland (£8),
Rowland Reyles (£8),
Philip Andrews (£8),
John Gryme (£7),
Nicholas Morris (£7),
Nicholas Garde (£7),

John Hobbes (£7),
Jamy Fallyke (£7).

There were 32 others, including some women and a Dutch alien widow, assessed from £6 to £2.

D
THE POOR in Tudor Times

In the mid sixteenth century, there was an increase in the number of men from the mainland moving around the Island looking for work, or simply looking for subsistence. The legal provision against vagrancy dated back to the Act of 1388. The parish officers would normally see their duty as helping such a man to move on, fearing that the vagrant would acquire the right to long - term support at the expense of the parish. Indeed an element of economic depression across the country made this a national problem, no longer since the Dissolution eased by charity centred on monastic houses.

With the suppression of the monasteries, it was the parish which was made responsible for the poor unable to work, and a start was made in setting to work the beggar who was capable of work, and a further attempt at penalties against able-bodied vagrants was made. Branding of those who refused work could reduce a man to slavery. In 1572 the office of Overseer (of the Poor) was created, effectively elected by the Vestry, though formally appointed by the Justices of the Peace. Later, parishes were allowed to levy a poor rate.

The basis for administration of the law for some two centuries was the act of 1601, late in the reign of Elizabeth, and confirmed early in the reign of her successor. It divided the poor receiving public relief into three categories: the able-bodied (who were to be found work), those who were unable to work (the impotent poor) and people who were deemed to be refusing to work. Poor rate was to be collected within each parish and here the churchwardens were key figures, though often helped by two substantial farmers or other landholders.

The rate was for four purposes:

'for setting to work the children of all such whose parents shall not be thought able to maintain them';

'for setting to work all such persons, married or unmarried, having no means to maintain them, and who use no ordinary or daily trade of life to get their living by'; (able-bodied pauper)

'for providing a convenient stock of flax, hemp, wood, thread, iron and other ware and stuff to set the poor on work':

'for the necessary relief of the lame, impotent, old, blind and such other among them being poor and not able to work'.

The poor rate was quite separate from alms collected in church, and the endowment set up as a charity by a local benefactor usually by will.

In punishing and deterring those who were deemed to be refusing to work, the Tudor period gives many examples which might well be regarded in the days of the welfare state as barbaric: in addition to branding on the shoulder there are cases of the hand being cut off, and even of death by flogging. These show both the desperation and the inability of the authorities to deal with the problem of economic depression and poverty.

FIVE
MANORS AND ELIZABETHAN DEFENCE

The Manors on the Island survived rather longer than on the mainland, and their names remain to the present.

Bagwich was a tenanted sub-manor of Apse in Tudor times, with the house delapidated, but the land provided a living for a yeoman farmer. In 1709 Bagwich Manor was owned by Thomas Rice, descendent of John Rice who a century before was Lord of the Manor of Bathingbourne, both estates being within Godshill parish.

Successive Lords of Godshill Manor were the Abbey of Lyra, the Monastery of Sheen, and Walsingham.

Bridge Court Manor had an important Mill on the River Eastern Yar during the 13th, 14th and 15th centuries. Wheat and flour not needed in the locality was exported through Wootton quay both to the mainland and across the Channel.

There was also a Water-mill at Appelford Manor, certainly in the 14th century. The Manor passed from Fitz-Azor through de Insula to Lisle. The fertile land of the Manor was in Tudor and Stuart times tenanted by a succession of Yeoman farmers, the Lisle family residing in Wootton. They retained the Manor House when they later sold the land to the Worsleys of Appuldurcombe.

At Sandford and Week Manors (held with Appuldurcombe Manor) the succession from the Conquest was Redvers, Montesbourg, Minoresses, possibly Sheen Monastery, Leigh & Worsley. As the Domesday Book confirms, there were also mills in the 11th century

As a general rule, mills survived for centuries on the same site, and the parish of Godshill continued both to grow and to process through the mills a substantial part of the cereal crop of the Island. In 1781 Sir Richard Worsley was to write in his history of the Island that 'large quantities of grain and flour (are) shipped for France, Spain, Portugal and ports in the Mediterranean Sea, with a considerable inland and coasting trade to Ireland and all the English Ports around the Channel. Such is carried on in wheat, flour, barley and malt.' He added that 'the Island, being naturally fertile, well-cultivated and not over-populous, even the thinnest crops afford a surplus of corn for the supply of foreign and other markets.'

Stenbury Manor was owned from the 11th century after the de Aula family by the Norman family de Heyno. The first of that family on the Island had married into the de Aula family and acquired ownership of Stenbury about 1100. A very old flat gravestone, unmarked save for a raised cross, on the right of the path as one ascends the path from the west to the church porch, is either 13th or 14th century (Bloxham's Companion). Tradition has it that this marks a de Heyno grave. In the 14th century a de Heyno was prominent in the military defence of the Island as is attested by surviving documents. Peter de Heyno led the raising of the siege of Carisbrooke Castle by the French in 1488. Shortly afterwards the owner of Stenbury Manor was Thomas Heyno, who had half a century earlier been pardoned by Henry VI for his treasonable acts as a young man. He had obtained Crown licence to maintain a private chapel for the family within the manor house.

In 1505 Thomas Heyno died leaving no son, and this fact altered the history of the manor. The de Heyno name died out and the family connection with Stenbury was shortly to end. Later Lords of the Manor were Beauchamp, Pound and Radclyffe Earl of Sussex. (One of Thomas Heyno's five daughters was not of legal capacity through mental disability. The accounts of Crown lands (1507) include as Royal income her rents and as Royal expenditure her 'mete and drinke' for 52 weeks, and 'kyrtylles smokks and kerchowes and other necessarie gere'. She is described uncompromisingly as 'ideot'). The other four de Heyno daughters were co-heiresses.

The eldest daughter was Mary (the wife of William Pound). Her quarter share in the estate passed on her death to her son Anthony and on his death without issue, to her daughter Honora. Honora had married Sir Henry Radclyffe, 4th Earl of

Sussex (openly a supporter of Queen Mary), and her son the 5th Earl on inheriting the share in the Stenbury Estate, sold it to Sir Robert Worsley of Appuldurcombe.

Thomas Heyno's daughter Elizabeth, with the agreement of her second husband Richard Dowee, sold her quarter share to John Welbeck and others, who were acting (either as known trustees or as covert nominees) for the Worsley family.

The share of Agnes, wife of Thomas Wyber, for reasons now unknown was conveyed to the man who married her grand-daughter: one Stephen Garat, and in 1565 he sold the share to John Worsley of Appuldurcombe.

The fourth share had been inherited by Katherine, and by 1580 that share too had passed to the Worsley family. Thus the property finally passed from a family prominent for the first four centuries after the Conquest in both Godshill parish and the Island, to a family to be prominent for some three further centuries. Such is the continuity of history.

Stenbury Manor was thereafter farmed by tenant farmers, and among them the Legge family. Before removal in 1923, there existed two early 17th century table-tombs near the south boundary wall of Godshill churchyard, one of Elizabeth wife of John Legge of Stenbury Manor, and a slightly later one dated 1641 of Richard Legge (perhaps their son). William Legge of Stenbury was an executor of the Will of John Worsley who died in 1580 (see section 11).

In the earlier years Stenbury Manor House was a moated castellated building, appropriate for those wilder times. In 1727, when the occupiers as part of major changes were digging to obtain soil to fill in the moat, they unearthed ten objects. These were earthenware cremation urns with some remains of coals and fragments of human bone, which could only mean that this site was pre-Christian, probably early Anglo-Saxon.

***

On the death of the popular Sir Edward Horsey, the Queen appointed as Captain of the Island another 'overner', Sir George Carey, eldest son of Baron Hunsdon, cousin of the Queen. His wife was Lady Elizabeth, described by Sir John Oglander as 'a lady as high minded as her husband, for she regarded but three ladies on the Island as suitable associates.' The Careys were strict Protestants, Spartan in style, and zealous to defend the Island from invaders. He issued rules restricting personal movement about the Island, curtailed trading, limited selling of land and goods, placed restrictions on borrowing and lending and controlled felling of timber. A total ban was placed on export to the mainland of farm produce and livestock, except under his personal licence. One could not even cross the Solent or go fishing without his permission.

When a compliant Minister in a prayer before the sermon in Newport called the Captain 'Governor', the complaints at his autocratic style turned to political action. A written Petition to the Queen's Council demanded that 'Freedom' be restored to 'her Majesty's faithful subjects'. The plea concluded: 'We find ourselves much grieved with the greedy and insatiable desire of some persons to get our lands and rightful possessions.' This petition was not the action of radical hot-heads, and indeed Thomas Worsley of Appuldurcombe and John Mewys of Bridge Court were among the signatories. The response of Sir George was predictably bellicose and accused the petitioning parties of 'mutiny at a dangerous time'. The desired result was however achieved in the sense that the powers of the Captain were never afterwards exercised in respects under complaint.

A particular area of concern was the attempt by Sir George to introduce legal formalities controlled by an Attorney in respect of business contracts and Wills. This was seen by the islanders as an affront to their honesty and integrity, and indeed to the ways of their forebears. As Sir John Oglander wrote with some hyperbole: 'Our ancestors lived here so quietly and securely, being neither troubled by London nor Winchester, so they seldom went out of the Island .... They always made their Wills, supposing there to be no trouble that was like to cause travail'. A Resident Attorney was for the first time ever introduced to the Island, but soon departed again. In colourful terms, Sir John Oglander suggested that he was 'hunted out of the Island . . . with a pound of lighted candles hanging out of his breeches . . . (and) with bells about his legs'. However, there were certainly changes, and Sir John Oglander was by 1627 pessimistic at their effect. 'The Isle of Wight is infinitely decayed', he wrote, and it was the introduction of the attorneys and the litigation that followed that he chiefly blamed. 'The Law has beggared us all.' Sir George Carey had become on the death of his father in 1587 both Lord Hunsdon and Great Chamberlain, and finally resigned as captain of the Island.

***

In 1588, as the likelihood of invasion in force by the Catholic powers of Spain and France was widely accepted, an elaborate system of signalling was put in place. Beacons manned by watchers were set up on the tops of Downs all around Godshill and over the Island. (This practice is documented from the 12th century when an inquisition was presided over by the two keepers of the ports and maritime lands of the Island.)

Two men manning each Beacon (including Appuldurcombe) had clear instructions to maintain watch round the clock.   On the enemy fleet being spotted, a prearranged signal was to be hoisted, and each other station would on sight of a signal do likewise. One watcher was then to run to the nearest Church (such as Godshill) and clash a Church bell. The other was to run to tell the local Justice of the Peace (such as at Appuldurcombe House).   The volunteer soldiers on the Island would be brought to 'stand-by' in battle order with cannon, to await further orders. As soon as the signals were seen on the mainland, soldiers were to embark in 37 boats to be ferried across the Solent, a single crossing being capable of moving 1,186 men. Local gentry with strategic responsibility were to take up position around the coast of the Island.

The Watchers were paid (8d a day), and were forbidden to have dogs with them for fear of being distracted from their duty. One assumes they were local men. The

Justices of the Peace had a continuing responsibility to check the signalling system regularly, and to ensure that any hut provided did not have seating, which was assumed to tempt the watchers to idleness. Surviving records show, albeit from later (1635), that two Scottish soldiers were billeted at Lavenders Farm, at the foot of 'Beacon Alley', Godshill. There was then an Officer in charge of the Beacon Guard.

Spain was the most powerful nation in the world and the richest. In due course the Spanish Armada set sail from Spain. The rendezvous of the fleet under Admiral Medina Sidonia, with the troop-carrying ships of the Duke of Parma was to have been off the Isle of Wight, though this was not known to the English authorities. On the 29th July 1588 (new style calendar) the expected Armada Fleet was sighted off the Lizard Point in Cornwall. The news swiftly spread. Sir Francis Drake took to sea from Plymouth to harass the powerful forces. On the 3rd August, those many Godshill people watching from the top of Appuldurcombe and Stenbury Downs saw the imposing but alarming spectacle of the long-rumoured enemy fleet. They assumed that the soldiers would be disembarked onto the beaches of the Island to occupy it as a base to attack the mainland.

The craft under Drake's command were smaller but more manoeuvrable and so better suited to the conditions, and the Spanish Galleons were harried ever eastwards in a series of skirmishes. Sir George Carey, Captain of the Island, said: 'Despite a great expense of powder and bullet, there have not been two of our men hurt.' The Island and mainland alike were spared the feared invasion.

Prayers of Thanksgiving for Deliverance were offered in Godshill Church as throughout the Realm, and with the name of Queen Elizabeth was joined those of Lord Howard of Effingham and Sir Francis Drake.

In 1603 the Queen died. Sir John Oglander expressed in his diary a view no doubt widely shared on the Island: 'Queen Elizabeth was one of the noblest, generous, bravest princes that ever lived and reigned in England. She had learning and wisdom . . . she was valorous above woman, and composed of stately gravity that was far from pride. Witness her affability even to the meanest of her subjects, a great favourer of learning and virtue; there was nothing wanting that could be desired in a Prince, but that she was a woman. England was richer, in better repute and esteem among foreigners, and every way the subjects more happy in her reign than ever they were before, or to be doubted ever will be again.'

E
VILLAGE TRADESMEN

Although many things which we today purchase, were in earlier times made within the home or simply not available, nevertheless there were many tradespeople in a village the size of Godshill. Some would be 'part-time' alongside a small-holding, or as one person in a household where others had other occupations.

The Alehouse Keeper at the sign of the Bell. Public Houses with this sign are nearly always near the Parish Church, and such was the case in Godshill. One writer of the time was critical of the use made of an establishment such as this. 'The true and principled use of Inns Alehouses and victalling hostels is two-fold, either for the relief and lodging of way-faring people travelling from place to place about their necessary business, or the necessary supply of the wants of such poor persons as are not able by greater quantities to make their own provision of Victuals. An alehouse is not meant for entertaining or harbouring of lewd or idle people to spend or consume their hard-earned money there.'

The Bakehouse. An oven would be kept in the village on the basis that one could either purchase a loaf made by the Baker, or for a small payment bake one's own food. The larger household and farm would not need this facility, but it made better economic sense in a village for one or two bakehouses to serve communally the cottagers, many of whom would not have an oven. A bakehouse would at Godshill be in the Street.

The Dairy. Until less than a century ago, each village would have several places where milk could be purchased, for it is not a commodity which travels well. Many a farmhouse would have its dairy, but small-holders too would keep a cow or two in milk. Moreover, cheese was a fairly cheap source of nourishment.

The Butcher. Although the poorer family would not see meat on their plates more than once a week, in the days before refrigeration many animals would be slaughtered and butchered locally, and only a larger farm would deal with these processes on the premises. For retail purposes the butcher needed to be in the centre of habitation. However, the cottager who kept a pig would deal with these matters himself with help from neighbours.

The Shoemaker/Cordwainer/Cobbler. Boots and shoes were made locally. Where most people walked, and surfaces were muddy or dusty and rough, footwear did not last long but was essential to health and reasonable comfort. The leather would have been prepared somewhere on the Island.

The Carpenter and Builder would be present in every community.

The Blacksmith and Farrier was a central figure in any rural community, and there might well be more than one forge in Godshill. Horsemen or their boys would lead horses in from the farms for shoeing, and the forge was a centre of horsemen's talk and of children's wonder. Farm implements would also be both fabricated and repaired locally. The Blacksmith was a man of status, and a recipient of confidences.

Other trades supporting the agriculture would be the Wheelwright and the Sawyer, though they would not need to be in the village itself.

SIX
INFORMATION from TAXATION RECORDS

Subsidy Rolls

The taxes in Tudor and Stuart times known as Subsidies provide a useful indicator of the better-off inhabitants of a parish. The record was kept not in a book but on a Roll, and many such rolls have survived. We are here concerned with the light the surviving records shed on the social structure of Godshill rather than the Subsidy itself. Too much should not therefore be read into the figures. The rates of tax varied from time to time, which makes comparison difficult, and that may possibly be compounded by evasion, which was a factor in tax-gathering at that time.

1526   the first Subsidy. 17 residents were assessed to give a total of £12.10.0d. Nine were on 20/-, six on 10/- and one each on 7/- & 3/-.

One of those taxed was the Vicar Thomas Bayly living in the Chantry Priests House. John Fry (son of Agnes wife of Sir John Leigh) held Appuldurcombe Estate as lessee of the Aldgate Convent.   The Fry family also held Godshill Park. Appleforde & Roud manors were held by Sir William Lisle of Wootton. One of the assets of the Appleforde estate was an ancient chapel called 'Nawdlyns' (chaplain Thomas Hall). (The Lisles founded another chapel in 1536 called 'Halydon'.) Bathingbourne Manor was owned by Mary Lisle, but she resided outside Godshill Parish. The tax-payer on Bagwich Manor Estate was probably Mr Baskett who had acquired Apse manor in Newchurch. Bridge Court estate was at this time growing commercially, and belonged to the Meux family, of whom Sir John Mew of Kingston was described by Sir John Oglander as 'an honest man, destitute of learning and a clounish sort of man'. Kennerly a new manor at this time was named after the family who farmed there.

1543   the list contained 113 names in Godshill, but the death of King Henry led to the aborting of that Subsidy.

1549   27 residents were assessed, and the total was £301.6.5d. The two Worsleys - Richard & Lady Anne (nee Leigh) - paid in aggregate £33.6.5d. Three others paid £18 each, 18 paid £10 to £12 each, and four between £7 & £5 each.

1570   63 residents were involved. John Worsley's assessment was £60, with two being assessed at £20 each, and 28 at varying levels between £13 & £4 each, and 32 less. Nicholas Garde of Kennerly was on £8 and John Love of Itchall on £3. The total was £388.

1594   The assessment totalled £242 from 37 Godshill inhabitants. Thomas Worsley was on £40, and Thomas Mews of Bridge Court and one other were on £12 each.   22 were on various levels from £10 to £4 (among them Peter Garde of Kennerly), and 12 on £3.

1597 yielded £185 from 31 payers. Thomas Worsley was again on £40, and Thomas Mew of Bridge Court and one other on £10 each.

1606 first Stuart Subsidy. Thomas Worsley's widow had re-married Sir Richard Whyte: £20. 29 others were listed for sums between £6 and £2, including John Rice of Bagwich Farm. The total from 30 was £127.

1610 on 27 residents, to total £106, made up of Sir Richard Worsley at £12, 9 at £7 to £4 including Peter Garde of Kennerly & John Serle of Saynham Farm, and 17 at £3.

1622 43 assessments were made in the parish, the highest (name not available) at £6, 7 (including Francis Worsley) at £5, 22 (including John Lavender) at £4 to £2, and 13 (including Richard Mew of Bridge Court & Alexander Lavender) at £1 each, total £123.

1641 at a time when the King and Parliament were on collision course. 40 parishioners were assessed, and paid £81. Sir Henry Worsley was on £10, 16 others (including John Lavender) between £4 & £2, and 23 (including The Revd Henry Worsley and Alexander Lavender) on £1.

1665 A post-Restoration Subsidy was the last of this type of taxation. Sir Henry Worsley of Appuldurcombe was assessed at substantially more than any other resident, namely £25, with six (including William Urry) on £3/£2, and 17 assessed at £1 (including Thomas Lavender). 24 assessments yielded £59.

In addition to Appuldurcombe, there were within the parish several smaller estates including Bagwich, Week, Sandford, Appleford, Roud, Rookley, Godshill Glebe, Bathingbourne and Lessland. Different rates were charged on the value of land from the level on goods and other wealth. Perhaps the most surprising fact to emerge is the fluctuating fortunes of the twenty or so most affluent gentlemen farmers and others, in relation to each other.

Hearth Tax

The Hearth Tax (popularly called 'chimney money') was a new rough-&-ready way of levying a differential tax on what was simple to see and difficult to conceal. Steady prosperity had led to substantial improvement of housing at all levels of society. Larger houses enjoyed greater comfort from several hearths with associated chimneys. Humbler dwellings had a hearth or two, each with a flue in a brick-built chimney. Nationally Hearth Tax was levied from 1662 to 1689 at 2/- a hearth, in two instalments a year. It was payable by the occupier, though in a widened sense of that word. Exemptions could be certified for those inhabiting dwellings worth less than 20 shillings a year not paying parish rates, and charitable & industrial establishments.

Godshill Parish was divided into five Tythings. This is an ancient word meaning originally a unit of ten households. (It has nothing to do with the tenth part of produce payable.) The word 'tithingman' or 'tytheman' denotes a petty constable with minor duties about this small unit of government. William Sefard signed

Hearth Tax returns in Godshill in that capacity. The unit larger than the parish was still the hundred. The Island was divided administratively by a boundary roughly on the line of the river Medina, whose name may simply have come from an old word meaning 'middle'. We also find it in the form Mede, Medham & Medine. It was then Sefard's responsibility to account to the High Constable of the Hundred of East Medina. Over a period several different ways of collecting the tax were tried, involving the Clerk of the Court for the whole Island: the Knights' (or Knighten) Court. Our present concern is the social information the records provide.

Some of the records are incomplete through age and wear, but even they yield much detailed information. Foremost names in the earlier period are given: Sir Henry Worsley (Appuldurcombe - 19 hearths), Alexander Lavender, John Lavender, Peter Garde, the Coleman family (Lancelot, Thomas, William, Elizabeth, Robert, Jane), Thomas Legg, Mr Harrison (Vicar), John Chesell, Richard Brown, Sir Robert Dillington, Richard Holbrook, Philip Casford. There were many exemptions.

In **1674** other names appear, such as:
William Sanders, Henry Ruffing, Capt Price & Edward Eaton.

We would hope to learn the comparative sizes of the Tythings, in terms of taxable dwellings (omitting the exempt properties) for example at 1665 & 1674. It is however difficult to interpret the figures: Weeke including Appuldurcombe (37, 24). Godshill (28, 12), Rookley (25, 25), Stenbury (15, 13), Rowd (8, 30). No sufficient explanation of the sharp shifts in three of the Tythings can be found. Only one new building is known: Henry Kingsland in Rookley. Some dwellings were noted as unoccupied and a few as having fallen into ruin, but not in such numbers as to explain the variations. An Exemption Certificate would be in standard form. Here is an example of the text:

"We the Minister of the Parish of Godshill in the Isle of Wight, and Church Wardens of the said parish doe hereby certifie unto His Majesty's Justice of the Peace for the said Isle That we doe believe That the respective Houses wherein the persons hereunder named doe inhabit are not of greater vallue than twenty shillings per annum upon the full improved rent, And that neither the person inhabiting, nor any other using the same messuages hath, useth, or occupieth, any lands, tenements, goods or chattels, of the value of Ten Pounds in their own possession, or in the possession of any other, in trust for them. And that the said Houses have not above two Chimneys, Fire-Hearths and Stoves in them respectively.
                    Witness our hands this 27th day of December,
                        one thousand six hundred and seventy
                        Signed   Ro Harrison,   Vicar
                                    John Wallis
                                    Tho Gaulton, Church Wardens"

It appears that one obvious and popular method of evasion was to sub-divide a dwelling into two or three 'separate' dwellings. To counteract this, a later addition was made to the form of these certificates to deal with any such evasion by sub-division after 1663.

An official list of inhabitants of the parish of Godshill has survived from 1665 to whom these Certificates of Exemption were issued. It is endorsed by the Overseer: "We allow of this certificate containing 58 names."

***

Much has been written on the movement of men and indeed households from one parish to another on the mainland in the early modern period, when the only means of travel on land was on foot, horseback and horse-drawn vehicles. It is perhaps inevitable that the barrier afforded by a stretch of several miles of water would make the population of the whole Isle of Wight more stable, and might also tend somewhat to reduce movement between parishes on the Island. There might indeed be a continuation of such tendencies into the twentieth century.

It is not therefore surprising to find that many surnames of Godshill Parish residents listed in the Hearth Tax records of the seventeenth century are still found on the Island 300 years later. (This short note is not an attempt at genealogy, but suggests that the modern interest in tracing descent may be substantially easier for some of those interested in the following surnames, particularly where they are not common on the mainland.)

Baker,	Downer,	Mew,	Stevens,
Biles,	Dyer/Deyer,	Morgan,	Stone,
Blow,	Hales,	Morris,	Thomas,
Browne,	Hart,	Orchard,	Thorne,
Burt,	Harvey/Hearvey,	Pittis/Pitts,	Urry,
Callaway,	Hollis,	Rayner,	Woodnutt,
Cheeke,	Hunt,	Reynolds/Renolls,	Whitehead.
Combes,	Joliffe,	Rolfe,	
Cooke,	Legg,	Saunders/Sanders	
Davis,	May,	Scovell/Scevell,	

F
THE BIBLE IN ENGLISH and CHURCH MATTERS

It is difficult for us today to re-live the impact that was made upon the minds of Godshill people when the Bible was made available to them in 1538 in their native tongue. For centuries the Scriptures had been in Latin. This meant that those few people educated in that tongue had a monopoly in selecting and explaining to the populace the riches of scripture. In a place like Godshill, that meant in practice the parish priest. In the Reformation, men sought to remove anything they considered to be an obstacle between them and God. In previous generations direct access to the Bible was considered dangerous for the uneducated; now it was held by many to be a basic right.

The earlier translation of the scriptures by Wycliffe was not widely available. Then Tyndale and Coverdale produced their translations, and by 1611 the Authorised or King James Bible was more generally in use. The task of the parish priest was to teach reading, and the material mostly read was the Bible. The result was that men and women began to ask questions and reason for themselves where a few generations earlier they had been obliged to accept what they were told by their priest and those few others who could read Latin.

For many years attendance at the Sunday Mass was virtually compulsory. On Sunday, businesses were closed, and all but essential work stopped. Even outside the hours of worship, games and most kinds of leisure were banned. Children were threatened with the devil when they ran or loitered in the lanes or fished in the brooks or played in the barns. Holy days were a source of conflict between those who wished to keep them similar to Sunday, and those who desired freedom from such restriction. The services were dominated by the voice of the priest alone, with a server to make the responses.

Those who absented themselves without sufficient reason were liable to be fined. It was the task of the vicar to see to the enforcing of the obligation. This would involve the collecting of fines, and reporting persistent offenders to the Consistory Court of the Bishop of Winchester. In some circumstances that Court might pass down a sentence of excommunication, in which case it was the duty of the Vicar to execute that decision also. It is highly likely that some of the higher ranks of Godshill society were periodically or even persistently absent from Church, but perusal of the Consistory Court records gives only the names of the poor and powerless, such as John Cook, Radigan Spanner and Elinor Knight.

Later, incumbents themselves were subjected to measures designed to remove those who could not see their way to accept the prevailing directives, and those who declined were removed from office. It may be significant that in the years from 1602 to 1660 there were a total of six vicars of Godshill, whereas from 1661 until 1734 there were only two.

SEVEN
GODSHILL SCHOOL to C 1815

In later medieval times it was normal for the ordained clergy to be regarded as the natural teachers of the young. Gentry wishing to make a gift to their locality, which would also ensure that their name was remembered, would think in terms of education, as well as the poor. Independently of this, there was also the desire to ensure gracious passage in the world beyond the grave by endowing a post for a priest to sing masses for the soul of the departed and for those he loved. In order to celebrate mass, the priest needed an altar either in an existing consecrated church or in a chapel newly erected for the purpose. Both required royal licence. It was not unusual for the priest to be given combined duties of chanting masses and running a small school, and such was the gift of the benefactor in Godshill.

Late in the 15th century Sir John Leigh married Dame Agnes (Appuldurcombe widow), who brought to the marriage that leasehold estate, and her rights as co-heir of John Hackett of Wolverton. The Hackett family are believed to have had the use of the south transept at All Saints as a chantry chapel. Certainly in 1520, just before the upheaval of the English Reformation, Sir John Leigh took possession of that chapel and endowed it afresh with an annual pension for a priest, on whom he placed additional teaching duties. A Report sometime before 1527 stated:

'The incumbent of the Chantry School is one John Griffiths, Master of Arts of the age of 40 years and hath £6 pension out of Hales Monastery . . . who teacheth there grammar to many young children.'

This may be regarded as the start of a Grammar School in Godshill for imparting a traditional Classical education. The method of securing the annual payment was to make a lump sum payment to a suitable institution which then guaranteed the payment, and perhaps provided the priest from among its number.

The arrangement in its original form was short lived, for the Chantries Act of 1547 in the first year of the reign of Edward VI suppressed chantries, as a few years previously the state had dissolved monastic houses. The question of the use of funds arising from the suppression of chantries was vehemently addressed by Hugh Latimer (1485 - 1555). He wrote: 'Here I will make a supplication that ye would bestow so much to the finding of scholars, of good wits, of poor man's sons, to exercise the office of salvation, relieving scholars, as ye were wont to bestow in pilgrimage matters, in trentals,[2] in purgatory matters.' There was some transfer of chantry revenues to the founding and maintenance of Grammar Schools (as well as other improvements within the church), although in practice too little of the Chantry endowments nationally escaped the private grasp of those who were favoured by the Court of Augmentations.

---

[2] Singing of 30 Masses in one day.

It was under this closure by law, that Lady Anne Worsley (widow, and daughter of the founder of the Chantry) was moved to act. The endowment reverted to the family, legend has it as a result of her petition to the ailing Henry VIII. Certainly the funds became available to Lady Anne to re-found the school. Moreover, by her Will, Lady Anne Worsley gave 20 Marks 'for the erection of a Free Grammar School in Godshill' to be served by a priest who would continue to reside at the Chantry Priest's House built by virtue of Sir John Leigh's Will. The School was held in part of that Chantry House 'a buttressed stone building' situated 'at the turning of the road to the South of the Church'. Local children were to be taught free of charge the elements of English Grammar and the rudiments of Latin and Greek.

In 1549, the Crown granted the old Chantry Priest's House to William Winnlow and Richard Field. These men are not named a few years later as local residents (Lay Subsidy Roll 1565) and it is possible that they were the Crown appointments to be Trustees of the School. There were local Trustees too: among them John Casford of Kennerlee Manor. Sir Richard Worsley (who died in 1565) bequeathed to the Schoolmaster a sum of £5 as a token of his gratitude for the work, and, despite the absence of a building other than the house, it appears that the foundation made a promising beginning.

On his death in 1580, Sir John Worsley, described as 'a plain but worthy gentleman, a brave scholar and a most generous housekeeper' bequeathed 40 shillings to Anthony Byrteswell the Schoolmaster of Godshill. In 1593, 9 Trustees were established, who agreed to pay certain rents as endowments to the school with provision in the event of death.

At the accession of King James I the school seems to have been growing in size despite the absence of an adequate building. The messuage consisted of 'the Chantry House in which the Free School was housed, an orchard and a garden house, the total value of which was £3'. In 1603 the Master was William Burbage. On his death, he too left a sum for the future development of the school: £15. By that time a second master (an Usher) was required to assist in the school.

Phillip Andrews, who died in 1604, by Will endowed the Free Grammar School with further money: £5 per annum to be paid to the Schoolmaster for the time being.

In 1607, John Rice, owner of Bathingbourne Manor, granted by deed to Sir Richard Worsley and the other trustees, ' a year's rent of 13/4d out of a close of ground containing 5 acres called 'Marles' in the Parish of Godshill on the east' to pay to the Schoolmaster of the Free Grammar School for the better maintenance of the school and him.' Later, in 1641, Thomas Rice sold the manor to Sir Henry Knollys, and in 1647 the latter confirmed the obligation in a deed to Sir Henry Worsley and 5 other trustees.

In 1615 Sir Richard Worsley gave a yearly sum of £11.6.8d, charged upon his Manors at Chale and Walpen. (It was not however the practice for the boys of the Worsley family to attend the school.)

In 1737, a 'temporary' schoolroom was built by parishioners at the Chantry House, which proved to be needed for 87 years.

By the end of the 18th century, there were two different legal foundations for boys in Godshill: the Tudor Grammar School giving classical education, and a Charity School for basic skills (the 3 Rs). They operated from the same premises. It was noted in the Vestry Minutes of 1794 'that the Free School and Guard Ushership are both vacant.' It was resolved 'that an Usher be appointed by the Parish at large, and approved by the Master of the Grammar School. That the *same person* (editor's italics) be appointed as Master of the Free School, by the Parish, and to enjoy the salaries of both, under the inspection of the Master of the Grammar School. That no person shall be permitted to become a Candidate who cannot produce a Certificate from creditable persons, of his sobriety and good character and who is of the Church of England'.

The same meeting provided that the Free School scholars should have four terms a year, breaking up at Easter for one week, at Whitsuntide for two weeks, at Harvest for four weeks and at Christmas for two weeks.

Twenty two years later, in 1816, when the Vestry appointed Thomas Finnemore Usher, the opportunity was taken to express rules, perhaps re-iterating existing ones, for what has to be thought of as a Parish elementary school, with a phantom Grammar School alongside. The children of the labouring poor were to be educated gratis. Others were to pay 10/6d per quarter if in addition to being taught to read, they were also to learn Writing and Cyphering (Arithmetic) etc. The quarterly charge for reading only was 7/6d. The decision who could afford to pay for instruction and who could not was to be made by the Minister, Churchwardens and Overseers. We note that these stipulations were being made over half a century before elementary education was made compulsory by Parliament in the 1870 Act. The Overseers were those Parish Officers in most direct contact with the poorer residents. The School building was to be appropriated every Sunday for teaching Catechism and other things in preparation for Confirmation under the direction of the Minister.

Despite the poor accommodation, in 1795 a Report had described Godshill School as 'at present in a flourishing and respectable state under the management of The Revd John Lancaster'. This was in contrast to many similar Grammar Schools in country districts on the mainland, where there was little demand for classical education. In the period 1750 to 1840, across the country many Masters drew their salaries from endowments without pupils to teach, since Trustees were obliged by law to limit the provision to classical education for which there was insufficient demand.

G
THE ECONOMIC SCENE - 17th Century

The scene in the Godshill parish at the opening of the 17th century was one of sheep roaming in large numbers over the Downs and on the common lands of the manors. Commoners would have rights of pasturage under local regulation. Pigs would run under the oak trees of more sheltered valley areas to consume the acorns. Yeoman farmers with small acreages from five to fifty were growing barley, wheat and oats, and also peas and beans (vetches). Their fields were on the whole not enclosed by hedges, but on the larger estates dry-stone walls were usual, and the remnants survive to this day. Orchards were numerous, and the popular drink was home-brewed cider.

Most cottages were built of locally-quarried stone, increasingly with chimneys and thatched. Plots were usually from one to three acres, giving ample ground for growing vegetables and fruit, though potatoes were not a recognised food at that time. A diet of rye-bread, bacon, mutton, peas & beans, and milk products would very likely be supplemented by mackerel and shell-fish, since local catches would be quickly moved both to markets and by travelling hawkers.

At this time, the cottager would use wooden platters, and rough earthen pots for drinking. Pewter was coming in, at least on the yeoman farms, and unglazed pottery might be fitted with a pewter rim.

The population of Godshill parish in the reign of James I was an estimated 550, of which perhaps 175 lived in the village itself, and these figures stress the relative importance of the farms and manors scattered throughout the parish. The population of the whole Island was about 15,500. Through the main street of Godshill there would have been clear front boundaries to the cottages and perhaps gardens, though probably not neatly aligned. Elsewhere, the highway was wide and often ill-defined, and the traveller would choose the route that afforded the least difficult passage according to the season and the prevailing conditions.

In wet weather, water poured down the three village chines from the higher ground, and ultimately found its way to the area known as the Munsley Bog.

***

One new factor in the early years of the 17th century among those disaffected with the lack of religious freedom was emigration to the 'New World'. For every one man or family that actually sailed, we may be sure there were a dozen who talked about it and considered taking the risk of a long journey into the unknown. The early settlers in what became New England were going to a primitive and inhospitable land, and there must have been much searching of souls and balancing of advantages and disadvantages. It was inevitable that those who sailed away were sturdy and independent men and women who gave up much in their native land as the price of the religious freedom that was so precious to them.

EIGHT
CLERGY & CHURCH MATTERS from 1603

Vicars of Godshill (1602 - 1734)

Andrew Byers/Bryars	1602 - 1611	
Arthur Price	1612 - 1617	
Edward Horden	1617 - 1629	
(son of Rector of Niton)		
Thomas Sanderson	1629 - 1639	
Thomas Cresfeld/Crosfield	1640 - 1652	
John Bushel	1652 - 1660	(Commonwealth)
Robert Harrison	1661 - 1700	(Restoration)
Barnabas Simson	1700 - 1734	(see below)
Thomas Shaw	1734 - 1735	

Queens College Oxford becomes Patron (1626)

During the reign of Queen Elizabeth, the right of presentation to the living of All Saints Godshill had become the possession of the Crown. Queen Henrietta Maria, wife of Charles I, was much involved in the support of Queen's College Oxford, founded nearly 300 years earlier. She obtained the transfer of various advowsons to that College.

"By the help of Thomas, Lord Coventry, Keeper of the Great Seal, Lord Hay, Earl of Carlisle; and George Goring, Vice-Chamberlain to the Queen; The Provost of the Queen's College Oxford got of the King, by the intercession of the Queen, the perpetual advowson and patronage of six churches in the County of Southampton viz the three Rectories of Hadleigh, Niton, and Weyhill, and the Vicarages of Milford, Godshill and Carisbrooke with the chapels of Newport and Northwood annexed. November the 12th 1626 AD"

We are not here concerned with the "price" for this grant: certain silver plate from the named churches, plate which incidentally was not owned by the patron but held in trust by the incumbent for the time being.

The Simson Family

The Revd Barnabas Simson came to Godshill as Vicar in 1700. It is not known where he and his wife Joanna lived, since there was no Parsonage house. All the following family entries were made and signed by him.

11th March 1700	"Barnabas Brooke Simson was born and christened"
6th March 1701	"Elizabeth, daughter of Master Simson, vicar, born".
12th March 1701	"Elizabeth baptised".
7th April 1703	"William, son of Master Barnabas Simson, born and baptised".
17th January 1704	"Jane, daughter of Vicar Barnabas Simson, born" (and later baptised).
20th November 1706	"Mary, daughter of Vicar Barnabas Simson was born" (and later baptised).

15th June 1708	"Charles, son of Vicar Barnabas Simson born" (and later baptised).
10th March 1712	"Joanne, daughter of Vicar Barnabas Simson born" (and later baptised).

(This, the 7th child born in 12 years, she was always referred to by her father as Anne.)

28th May 1714	"Joanna Simson, wife of the Revd Master Barnabas was buried".

Thus the father was left a widower with seven children aged between fourteen and two years of age.

7th April 1723	"Sarah, christened in Godshill Church".

This was the first of the next generation, the daughter of the Vicar's second son William, who had married probably at Newchurch, his wife's parish. The child died, probably also at Newchurch.

4th August 1727	"Judith was baptised, child of Mary Simson and Nathaniel Willis".
~ September 1727	"Mary, third daughter of the Vicar Barnabas Simson, was married, in the church to Nathaniel Willis".
11th January 1729	"Jenny was christened, daughter of Mr & Mrs William Simson".
Same date	"Nanne christened, daughter of Mary Simson and Nathaniel Willis".
24th January 1729	"Barnabas Brooke Simson, born 11/3/1700, died, 24/1/1729. 28 years of age". (This is the Vicar's eldest child.)
25th January 1731	"Mary, daughter of Mary Simson and Nathaniel Willis, christened".
7th September 1732	"Anne was married to William Hills". (This was the Vicar's youngest child.)
28th December 1732	"Provenaux, daughter to Mary Simson and Nathaniel Willis was christened at the font in Godshill Church".
15th December 1733	"A second Sarah was born to the Vicar's son William." (It

was a frequent practice to give a child the same Christian name as a deceased sibling.) Barnabas Simson performed the baptism ceremony of this grandchild on Christmas Day. He had completed the register in respect of all the above events.

14th February 1734	"Master Barnabas Simson Vicar of Godshill died".
18th. February 1734	"Master Barnabas Simson Vicar of Godshill buried in the churchyard".

Records show that Barnabas Simson preached up to the last Sunday of his life. The ceremony was conducted by Master John Shaw, temporary priest -in-charge.

On the outside of the west wall of the south transept of All Saints Church Godshill is the monument to Barnabas Simson, with a coat of arms carved on the base and two carved piles of books on the shoulders of the pediment, to indicate his learning.

<u>Whitwell</u> (see section 2)   Despite the dual ecclesiastical history, parochial rates were separately collected, and Whitwell was 'deemed' a distinct parish, but did not gain that status officially until 1867.

<u>Tithes</u>
In their purest form, tithe contributions had none of the characteristics of taxation, except that payment had been enforceable at law since late Anglo-Saxon times. From the viewpoint of the beneficed parish clergy, tithes (whether in kind or commuted by agreement into a cash payment known as a composition) were a vital element in the income which supported the post, known as a living. There was for centuries no payment from any central fund.

The income of the parish priest came from four sources:
tithes
from farming (or renting out) the glebe-land
from fees for certain specified services (the occasional offices) and
from freewill offerings for example at Easter.

Tithes were originally paid by all those with property or income within the parish, one tenth of annual produce, but the system became increasingly complex.

In the earliest days, tithe was for four objects considered desirable:
maintaining the fabric of the parish church, or perhaps just the chancel
maintaining the parish priest in his pastoral responsibilities
    (the cure of souls)
helping to maintain the wider church and
via the parish priest helping the poorest section of the parish community.

Gradually only the second of these was prominent. What had begun as a satisfactory system was increasingly felt as an unreasonable burden. Those in Government shied away from reforming the system for centuries after it ceased to be satisfactory. The fault was not so much in the individuals, as in the system, once the surrounding situation changed.

<u>Rector and Vicar</u>
First, how were they alike? Both were clergy presented to a living by a Patron, who owned that right of presentation as a piece of property, to be exercised whenever a vacancy arose. (The Bishop of the Diocese made the actual appointment and in theory could decline to appoint the man presented by the Patron.) Once inducted into the parish living, such a clergyman was entitled to the income of the benefice during his period of office, which frequently continued until death. He enjoyed security of tenure, known as the freehold, as well as fulfilling certain obligations of the office. Both a rector and a vicar were beneficed clergy. We are not here concerned with other clergy (unbeneficed) who might carry out the duties of parish priest without the benefit of the security or the status.

In the early Middle Ages, a parish church is to be thought of as an asset producing income. The patron had the right to present to the post which enjoyed that income. The amount of income varied considerably, but was frequently more than a single priest needed to live on, arising originally often out of the generosity of past ages.

The main difference between a rector and a vicar related to the right to the tithe income. Where originally the benefit was for the incumbent on the spot, the pious custom grew to give the right to receive the income of a parish (particularly the tithe) to a religious community (which became legally the 'rector'). That monastery or similar house then fulfilled the duties of the office by appointing a priest to act vicariously for it (which explains the term 'vicar'). The major crops received went to the monastic house after harvest, and the lesser were collected perhaps even daily by the vicar. At this stage, provided the monastic house exercised its rights responsibly, one might argue that the changed system did not damage the interests of the parishioners.

However, the system changed again at the Dissolution, for the right to collect rectorial tithes then often fell into the hands of a layman and became separated from any spiritual obligation. It became an investment, to be bought and sold, and often became separated from the advowson. The advowson was the patronage, the right to present a clergyman to the living when it fell vacant, but carried no right of ownership.

Plurality Not only the loss of tithes, but other factors and changes meant that the value of livings continued to vary considerably. Some would be insufficient to support the style of living thought to be appropriate to a parish priest, who might well have come from a gentry family and to have graduated from University. One obvious way for those with social influence to gain access to a gentry level of income was to take two livings, and employ a curate to serve one at a modest salary. Such a curate might be a young man awaiting his own incumbency, or someone of lower social status and expectations.

A patron who held the right of presentation of two parishes in the same area might well consider it appropriate to offer two livings together to one man, and the Bishop might well concur. This system of plurality was widespread in the eighteenth century, and not until the 1830s was the problem addressed.

This double income is the most likely reason for one man being both resident Rector of Niton and non-resident Vicar of Godshill, with a Curate serving Godshill as his employee, as was the situation from 1735 to 1867. The non - resident Vicars were:

William Thornton	1735 - 1751
William Wood	1751 - 1761
Isaac Knipe	1761 -1786
John Barwiss	1786-1828
Richard Dixon	1828-1858
George Hayton	1858-1867

(6 men: 132 years)

Their Curates (priests in residence) at Godshill included:

William Sewell, Joseph Lancaster, William Wilkinson, John Hurnall, Henry Worsley, Daniel Walsh & W L Girardot.

The parish of Godshill at that time extended across Stenbury Down & Rew Down to the coast at Steephill. It was bounded on the south & south-west by St Lawrence, Whitwell & Chale, on the west by Carisbrooke & Kingston, and on the north & north-east by Newchurch & Arreton (although Arreton parish extended close to the centre of Godshill village just north of Munsley Farm).

H
MAIL, RABBITS, MARKET AND BULL-BAITING

In Tudor times letters were conveyed across the Solent to and from the mainland by the 'coneyman'. He came over at short intervals by boat to purchase rabbit meat for sale in London, and carried mail by private contract as a lucrative 'side-line'. In 1615, however, the Royal mail was inaugurated.

Rabbits were prolific on Downs and in valleys alike, and snaring both for the table and for the skins was a regular source of income to islanders. If better prices could be obtained from the coneyman than for local consumption, so much the better.

The busy market in Newport provided an additional source of selling such produce. The town received borough status in the reign of James I. The Saturday Market was noted for its livestock. We have to picture St James's Square as a centre for the auction of sheep and cattle both for breeding and fattening, and for slaughter. Trade in horses too was brisk. The bustle and bargaining, the noise of the animals, the crying of wares and buzz of conversation, the muck and the crush: all were part of the scene. Around the Market the inns and taverns quenched the thirst and satisfied the hunger of village people who every week trudged to the Market from Godshill and similar places.

On holy-days there was likely to be 'sport', the baiting of a bull donated by an Island dignitary. Solidly embedded in the ground was the means of tethering the doomed animal in the Bull-ring, allowing him limited space for manoeuvre. Large crowds gathered to see the spectacle, and the Mayor and leading townsmen would be among them. The first dog to be loosed - 'the Mayor's dog' - was decorated with ribbons. Others in turn were released to attack the tethered bull, cheered or hooted at as appropriate. Wagers on the endurance of the animals were not restricted to the prominent gentlemen. When all the dogs had taken their turn, the signal was given for the maddened bull to be killed in the market-place and the meat distributed. It appears that on the Island no slaughter would take place until the creature had been baited in this way.

Godshill people could also attend bull-baiting in Brading, and the practice continued on the Island until banned by legislation in 1835.

Travel around the Island was for the great majority of Godshill residents limited to business such as going to market. Travel for pleasure was a rare luxury for those who could afford time from the business of gaining a living. Most walked, and the able-bodied who could afford to keep a horse would ride 'two up' for as long as could be endured by their mount. Each parish maintained its own highways, and in anything but good weather the picking of a reasonable passage made progress slow and arduous.

NINE
THE FIRST SIX APPULDURCOMBE BARONETS - 1603 to 1768

In a list of 46 gentlemen and farmers living on the Island compiled in 1610, Sir Richard Worsley of Appuldurcombe was second, above the Lord Chief Justice of England.

Needing to raise funds for a military campaign in Ireland, James I instituted a new rank of Baronet and the title was sold to Knights of the Realm. Thus Sir Richard Worsley became in 1611 the 1st Baronet, entitled to the abbreviation after his name (Bart or Bt). He was not only a Justice of the Peace but also from 1614 for the rest of his life Member of Parliament for Newport (IoW). King James had a low opinion of the value of the House of Commons, warning the members not to 'debate publicly the state matters that were far above their reach and capacity'. However, Sir Richard was not among the more rebellious of the Commons, associated as he was with those who had influence with the King at Court. Sir Richard attended the last Parliament of the reign in 1620/21.

Although he was a man ready to apply himself to public duty, when with his friends at leisure he had retained the boisterous ways of his youth. There are recounted tales of cushion fights and similar schoolboy behaviour, until it was pointed out to him that he was at risk of losing the sight of his remaining eye.

Sir Richard and Lady Frances had seven children, and he died in 1621 after returning to Appuldurcombe from public duties in London. Some members of the household had contracted smallpox. On entering the house, Sir Richard went to the children to enquire after their condition. Shortly afterwards he himself was taken ill, and died of complications after impatiently seeking to resume normal life. He was buried in the south Chancel of All Saints Church Godshill amid a show of exceptional grief. Sir John Oglander, a close friend, wrote of him as 'a man of learning, a patron of virtue, a friend of good companions, bestowing credit on his house and the Island'.

His widow Lady Frances was soon discovered to have passionate longings for a young bachelor in their social circle, Sir Charles Bartlett, but her feelings were not reciprocated. Sir Charles married a lady of his choice, arousing such jealousy in Lady Frances that she expressed her passion in verse:

Be what thou wilt, be counterfeit or right,
Be thou constant, serious, vain or light,
My love remains inviolate the same,
Thou canst do nothing that can quench the flame,
But it will burn as long as thou hast breath,
To keep it kindled, if not after death.

No one was there more true than I to thee,
And though my faith must now despis-ed be,
Unprized, unvalued, at the lowest rate,
Yet this I'll tell thee - 'tis not all thy state,
Nor all that's better and seeming worth of thine,
Can buy thee such another love as mine,
Liking it may be - but oh! - there's as much odds
Between love and liking as between men and their gods.

One result of this situation was a withdrawal of the support and interest in the community of Godshill and its Church that had previously been a feature of the Worsley family. Lady Frances then left the Island upon her second marriage. She became the wife of Colonel Jeremy Brett, Captain of the King's Guard at the Castle of Southsea on the mainland, and a relative of the infamous 2nd Duke of Buckingham.

Her eldest son Henry had succeeded in 1621 to the estate and baronetcy, as the 2nd Baronet. He too made a marriage to a lady of influential family, a daughter of Sir Robert Wallop MP, of Hampshire, who was to sit as a Judge during the trial of King Charles. Lady Bridget brought to the marriage the Manor of Chilton Candover (Hants) and it remained in the Worsley family until 1747. Sir Henry was one of the 18 gentlemen who were Justices of the Peace in the Knighten (Knights') Court. This Judicial tribunal dated back to the Norman Conquest with a strong feudal sense, that dispensing justice was a matter for the leading figures on the Island.

The Island was in 1625 under arms. One of the dozen or so bands was from Appuldurcombe with 9 Officers, 150 'Muskettes', 25 'Corslettes', 37 Bare 'Pickes' and 40 Men unarmed, some 261. The sum total of all the able men within the Island was given as 2020, with an added note that 'since they all are armed.' A Watch of 2 men was kept from Appuldurcombe (Down) under Sir Henry's command. When Lord Conway, Governor of the Isle of Wight, wished in 1628 to establish the order of military precedence of the commanders of the Militia, he named 'Barronnett' Worsley first in the eastern half of the Island (the East Medham).

Sir Henry himself was from 1640 Member of Parliament for Newport (IoW), in that time of great national turmoil. He was under the strain of having a mother strongly Royalist in sympathy, whilst his wife was earnestly Parliamentarian. Such divisions were by no means unusual across the land. Sir Henry's step-father Colonel Brett commanded a regiment in an unsuccessful expedition against the Scots in 1639, and indeed his life was under threat when his troops mutinied in Durham on their return to England. After the outbreak of the First Civil War in 1642, the Royalist Col Brett was appointed by King Charles I Captain of Carisbrooke Castle, and Lady Frances returned with him to the Island. The Castle came under siege by Parliamentary sympathisers. The initiative seems to have been taken by the townspeople of Newport under local leadership, but they were supported by some four hundred seamen who had come ashore from the English fleet lying off the coast of the Island. Col Brett had a mere twenty men-at- arms, and under his protection he had his wife and also the family of the former Captain of the Island the Earl of Portland. By way of provisions he had only three days' supply, and when able to obtain honourable terms he surrendered the Castle. Lady Frances did not live to see the Restoration, but died in 1659.

At the Restoration, Sir Henry returned to Parliament (this time for Newtown (IoW) in 1661, and his son took the seat after him. By the time Sir Henry died in 1666 after 45 years as Baronet his elder son Robert had married Mary Herbert the granddaughter of the 4th Earl of Pembroke who was under Parliament appointed Governor of the Island. The Herberts were a powerful and well-connected family from Buckinghamshire. Sir Robert, 3rd Baronet, was more a man of learning than a politician or farmer. He and Lady Mary were keen travellers on the continent. However, Sir Robert died in 1676 only ten years after his father, when his elder son also Robert was aged only 7, and it was agreed that the boy should be placed in the care of his uncle James Worsley, who also managed the estates. In 1690, when attaining his majority and taking up the Worsley estates and title as 4th Baronet, Robert married an heiress: the Hon Frances Thynne, daughter of the first Viscount Weymouth, a prominent public figure. The family seat was at Longleat. The young couple had in addition to the Appuldurcombe house and estate, similar properties in Chilton (Bucks) Hampshire and Wiltshire.

Under a prosperous Lord of the Manor at Appuldurcombe Godshill parish was also enjoying a time of peace from foreign invasion and incursion, and the period is marked by re-building of comfortable Manor Houses. The Island continued in its prosperity and with the social rise of the farming fraternity it was said that 'money was as plentiful in the yeoman's purse as in the gentry's pocket'. The Island stone was quarried from several sites, including Godshill, to build cottages as well as larger houses. The skill of stone-masons, thatchers, joiners and other craftsmen was widely deployed. A new import was roofing-slate from North Wales. Agriculture was both arable and animal husbandry, with sheep on the downs and commons, and pigs in the woodlands.

Sir Robert desired a settled home, and despite public duties at Westminster as MP for Newtown (IoW), was a countryman at heart. He promised his wife that he would build a mansion at Appuldurcombe to replace the Tudor Manor House now considered unfashionable and lacking in refined comforts. Sir Robert made a detailed sketch of the house as it was about 1690 and wrote, in exaggerated terms that he had 'not left one stone standing'. The mansion was situated a small distance from the original Priory House.

An unfortunate set-back came in November 1703, when a tremendous storm caused damage to the property. Archduke Charles of Austria (later to be Charles of Spain) was sailing or rather riding out the storm off the Island, and Sir Robert was compelled to excuse himself from entertaining Charles, much to the chagrin of Lady Frances who would have welcomed this indication of their status on the Island.

The preparatory work after choosing his Architect and agreeing the plans took some years, and it was presumably lack of funds which caused the postponement of laying of foundations. Sir Robert was a devout man, and among his friends was Thomas Ken then Vicar of Brighstone (IoW) but later the non-Juror Bishop Ken and remembered as hymn-writer. His Christian devotion explains why an early part of the project was the building of the chapel. Lady Frances wrote to her father: 'the chappell goes up apace' but she confesses to impatience for other progress, for she continues: 'I wish he (Sir Robert) would let them (the masons) go on as fast with the rest of the building that we might see an end of it which I hardly hope to do'. It must have been a trying time for a lady brought up in what we may term 'polite society'.

Much of the stone was greensand from the Undercliff on the south-east coast of the Island, with one supplier giving credit for old hewed stone from the earlier house. Local names appear among those digging and transporting stone, including a widow. Portland stone was imported from the mainland with freight charges more than doubling the 'quarry-gate' price. The carters were rewarded with 'two hogsheads of beer' and those supplying the beer were 'generously recompenced (with) tobacco and smoking pipes'. John Davis of Borthwood (IoW) supplied 30 quarters of lime. George Hart of Rookley was contractor for six dozen wattles, and John Davis supplied 850 feet of plank wood salvaged from a wreck. The deal scaffolding spars came from Sam Smith.

Sir Robert took a keen interest in the design of the gardens, sometimes it seems to the neglect of the building works. In this he was helped by the despatch of rare and exotic plants from distant lands by his younger brother Henry who, continuing their father's love of travel, visited many parts off the usual continental itinerary. It was in keeping with this that Henry was appointed Governor of Barbados under Queen Anne, and later Envoy to Portugal. He died a bachelor. The north Transept of Godshill Church (long previously a Chantry Chapel of the de Heyno family) was rebuilt at his expense and finally in memory of his brother too, and the south Porch was also built at about this time.

When Sir Robert died in 1747, he and his wife were childless, and it was his cousin from Pilewell (Hampshire) who succeeded him. Sir James, the 5th Baronet, was a man of considerable learning and an antiquarian, and his great contribution was to start to collect material for an intended history of the Isle of Wight. He had no interest in continuing the building work at Appuldurcombe, and living quietly in Hampshire, he made little social impact on Godshill. He died in 1756 and was buried on the mainland.

The 6th Baronet was Sir Thomas Worsley, son of James, who had married Lady Elizabeth the daughter of the Earl of Cork & Orrery, Baron Marston. Her father and grandfather moved in literary circles and in childhood she would have heard talk of the likes of Swift, Pope and Johnson and may indeed have met them. Again there was great contrast between the Baronet and his wife, for his great interest was in his command of the South Hampshire Militia. In the year he succeeded to Appuldurcombe, war broke out once more with France, and attacks and indeed invasion were once more a threat. Sir Thomas supervised the training and readiness of the Militia, but like his father did not live permanently in Godshill parish. A rough outspoken man, he engaged in a war of words with someone in that respect similar: the Duke of Bolton, Governor of the Island.

A visitor to Appuldurcombe was Sir Edward Gibbon the historian, and he was willing enough to share in the boisterous visits to local inns, where no doubt Sir Thomas was privy to the transactions of the smuggling fraternity who were so active at this time on the Island. Sir Thomas took no steps towards completion of the buildings at Appuldurcombe, and was not interested either in furthering the intended history of the Island. He did however agree to accompany his wife abroad on travels on the continent, and their journeys took them to wilder and more primitive parts of south Italy and Sicily than were normally travelled by English gentlefolk.

When Sir Thomas died in 1768 at the age of 40, he was followed by his son Richard, 7th Baronet Worsley.

I
TWO COLOURFUL WORSLEYS

The first Worsley at Appuldurcombe was James, who came from the north of England, and arrived on the Island in about 1516 (see section 3).

With him came his brother Giles Worsley with his 1st wife. He later settled at Ashey Manor, purchased at the time of the Dissolution. Giles had in turn no fewer than four wives, his fourth being from the prominent family Tichbourne, and by that marriage the elder of two sons was named Thomas. Giles died in 1558, leaving a Will which was disputed. The outcome was that the son Thomas, the first of our colourful Worsleys, took a two-thirds share of the Ashey Estate.

Thomas married a daughter of William Bowyer from Hampshire. Thomas was a most turbulent and unrestrained man, full of wild pranks. He was reckless with money, and careless of the family name. After separating from his legal wife, in her lifetime he 'married' his maid-servant.

There was one son of the marriage, given the first name Bowyer. The Earl of Holderness was 'patron' of Bowyer Worsley, and influenced a grant of knighthood to him. One of Sir Bowyer's children was a girl named Barbara.

A man named Thornton from Sussex came with his son to live on the Island though without a settled place of residence. Sir Bowyer Worsley and his family gave them hospitality at Ashey Manor. The Thornton son secretly married Bowyer's daughter Barbara. Both fathers took a strong line, Thornton senior sending his son away, while Sir Bowyer forced Barbara to remain at Ashey. There were several family meetings to try to resolve matters. Thornton senior demanded a settlement sum of £1000. Sir Bowyer was unprepared to pay more than £500. He finally agreed to settle for that sum then, plus a Bond for a further £500, on the explicit understanding that the balance under the Bond would never be claimed. At around this time, Sir Bowyer sold his properties including Ashey Manor.

Later the two Thorntons claimed on the Bond and went to law. Sir Bowyer stubbornly refused to pay and was arrested. He applied successfully to the Governor of the Island, Lord Conway, for an order for release from prison. In June 1629 he again successfully petitioned the Governor for a place on board a vessel lying off shore, which astute move gave him Crown protection against re - arrest. Having disposed of all his properties, Bowyer sailed across the Atlantic and settled in New England.

Thomas was nephew of the first Worsley of Appuldurcombe. Sir Bowyer Worsley was his great nephew.

TEN
BIRTHS, DEATHS AND MARRIAGES

It was the duty of the Incumbent both to keep a record of Baptisms, Marriages and Burials, and to read to the Congregation each Sunday any entry made during the previous week. The only relic of this latter practice today is the calling of Banns.

Pre-1812 Godshill Registers have survived in four volumes but are not complete.

Overall periods:
Baptisms and Burials   from 1678 to 1800,   and 1801 to 1812
Marriages only   from 1754 to 1791,   and 1791 to 1812
The incompleteness suggests that other records were kept separately from time to time, which have not survived.
Baptisms   1753 to 1798
Marriages   1769 to 1798
Burials   1737 to 1753 (all inclusive)
(The surviving Registers have now been transferred to Island archives at Newport.)

Summary of numbers

First period - 1678 to 1720 (inclusive)

Baptisms:

Average per year 21 in the years 1678 to 1706
fluctuating between 36 (1691) and 9 (1680),

Average per year 11 in the years 1707 to 1720
fluctuating between 21 and nil (1711)

No reason can be offered for the fall in numbers from 1707.

Marriages

Average per year 4
fluctuating between   10 (1687, 1690, 1702) and
                    nil (1683,1684,1695,1696,1700, 1709,1717,1718)

Burials

Average per year 11
fluctuating between   29 (1679) 28 (1690) & 26 (1689) and
                    nil (1720 & 1)(1717, 1719)

Highest number of deaths of children under 16 in a year: 8 (1690, 1691)

Second period from 1721

Baptisms 1721 to 1752 (inclusive)

Average per year 12
fluctuating between   28 (1736) and
                    3 (1744, 1745, 1747, 1749) 379 in total

Marriages 1721 to 1768 (inclusive)

Average per year 4
fluctuating between   11 (1755, 1757) and
                    nil (1721/24,1726,1729,1743/48,1750)

Burials 1721 to 1736 (inclusive)

Average per year 6
fluctuating between   18 (1731) and
                    nil (1721,1722,1723,1732)

***

The quality of the entries varies, most being formal and brief, but some Incumbents seem to have taken particular care, notably Barnabas Simson (Vicar from 1700 to 1734) The Register entries of his family are set out at Section 8.

Others add words, or the entry has an element of intrinsic human interest.
In 1678, burial of Mary the wife of Master Robert Harrison, Vicar.

In 1679, burial of George, son of Master Robert Harrison, Vicar.
In 1700, burial of Master Robert Harrison, Vicar

Earlier: 3rd February, burial of Richard Masters ... baseborn
11th February, burial of Joan Masters
(presumably died as a result of childbirth).

A few examples taken from the registers (1679 to 1705) make the point that children were frequently conceived before marriage, although in all these cases the mother's name is not given as the parent.

In one instance, a child was baptised on the same day as his father's marriage (1679). Later that year a child was baptised two day's after his father's marriage. 3 other pairs of entries show a child baptised 4, 5 & 7 months after the father's marriage.

It should be noted that at this time the legitimacy of the child was granted, provided that the birth took place within one month after the marriage of the parents. This was an interesting concession to human frailty which was designed to encourage maintenance within a stable family unit.

In 1709, burial of Joseph Read of Newchurch who was over 100

In 1754, burial of Sarah Bye from the Gun House. This was the dwelling where the cannon or fawconett had earlier been housed as part of the village defence against invasion. The cannon was sent to Loughborough bell-founders in 1813 to be melted down for re-casting.

In 1763, when Mary Dyer was buried, there is an additional note that this was the "first entry from ye Poor House", the parish provision for 'paupers'. Later the same year a child was buried "from ye Poor House".

What today we might call the Workhouse would have been a Parish institution, prior to the 1771 Island Act referred to at Section 14. The later name was House of Industry. Its site is remembered by the name of a Shute, part of the Shanklin Road eastwards out of Godshill.

Also in 1763, 18 days apart, two boys, presumably twins, "ye bastard infants of one Anne Symonds a married woman."

In 1770 and at other times, the burial entry of an infant is described by a term less extreme in our ears: 'natural son'.

In December 1778, within the space of 24 days, four burials in the family Jolliffe were recorded, aged 41, 40, 20 & 10, all having died of smallpox. It was 22 years later that Edward Jenner's experiments led to vaccination becoming an established and indeed obligatory procedure.

2nd November 1783 "John Fleming, who was found lunatic by a Coroner's Inquest, was buried. He was aged 55 years".

Urry as a cottage (now a ruin) which stood inside the Freemantle Gate the entrance to the Appuldurcombe estate. The 1979 Telephone Directory listed one Urry in Rookley, one in Godshill, and 9 elsewhere.

Speed

John Speed was subject to the Hearth Tax on 2 hearths (1674) in Godshill. There are then a number of Godshill Register entries relating to Speeds, up to 1793 (about 120 years). Thereafter, families of that surname lived in other parts of the Island.

Mew (earlier Meux)

Hearth Tax returns (1664/1673) show the Mew family in the Week area of the parish. One of the Speed daughters married a Mew in 1703. There are still Mews living in the parish.

Davis

If this is an anglicised version of a Welsh surname, it was perhaps introduced to the Island among the retinue of the Lords of Glamorgan who became extensive landowners, especially in West Wight. The Godshill parish Registers from 1678 to 1754 list 63 entries with that surname. The Hearth Tax records show material poverty, since four of the Davis surname had but a single hearth in each dwelling. Addresses where known are at and around Sainham Farm.

Morris

The Godshill Registers from 1678 to 1797 contain 35 entries with this surname. It appears that they lived at Pagham Farm in Godshill parish, at this time a rather poor holding probably attached to Budbridge manor.

Some surnames from the list of taxpayers in the reign of Queen Elizabeth I are familiar to local residents in living memory or even of our own day.
Harvey: in 2000 there was still a person with that surname in the village.
Lavender: perhaps the first to give his name to Lavender's Farm.
Legge, Cooke, Morris, White, Sanders, Blowe, Andrews. These surnames were still found in Godshill parish in the 1970s, possibly related. Also Coleman: of the Manor of Rookley; this surname continued to be familiar. For example, in 1631 Lancelot Coleman was Churchwarden of All Saints Godshill.

***

Christian names: although the Island was a long journey from the mainland, the choice of Christian names closely mirrored that over the whole kingdom.
Girls' names noted in Godshill registers between 1678 and 1752:
53% were christened Mary, Elizabeth or Ann(e) which is not dissimilar to their popularity in mainland England.

Jane, Sarah and Hannah were the three next most popular names on both the Island and the mainland.

Of boys' names, nationally John, William and Thomas totalled 56%. In Godshill parish the same three names totalled 47%, with Thomas being fourth most frequent behind James. Richard, Robert and Abraham were next most popular in Godshill.

In the year 2000 the congregation of All Saints Godshill still comprised two Marys, an Elizabeth, Anne, Jane, Sarah and Hannah, a John, James and Thomas.

J
WARS AND EFFECTS OF WARS (1627 - 49)

England had in 1627 drifted into war with France, for many and complex reasons, both commercial and religious. Unlike earlier wars, it was unpopular on the Island. The Duke of Buckingham, close associate of King Charles, was to lead an expedition to relieve the besieged Huguenot town of La Rochelle on the west coast of France by capturing the Isle of Rhe just off the mainland. His force was eventually some 10,000 men, but many of the lowest calibre were recruited, the very dregs of society.

About 1,000 of these were billeted on the Island for training in readiness to embark, and the lodging problem was solved by dispersing single companies of men to each of the larger villages. So strong was the reaction from Island residents that Sir John Oglander (Deputy Governor) travelled to London to protest to the King, but without avail.

The expedition was a complete failure. It resulted in ignominious withdrawal back to England, with many troops needing to be accommodated on the Island once more.

The most that Sir John Oglander succeeded in obtaining was some financial recompense for the Islanders, and a royal visit of inspection of the troops.

There was a second cause of complaint. Later, some 1,500 Scottish Highlanders of the Royal Scots Regiment, were also to be billeted on the Island. Records show that two were placed with Farmer John Lavender of Godshill in 1635. The stay on the Island lasted about a year, because the intended military initiative was postponed and with it any relief for local people. The soldiers, 'as barbarous in their nature as in their clothes' were beyond the control of their officers, and the consequence was 'murders, rapes, robberies, burglaries, getting of bastards and almost the undoing of the whole Island'. Appeals to the King's Council led to no satisfaction, except such as arose from a second royal visit. Only the despatch of another expedition to La Rochelle relieved the inhabitants.

Sir John Oglander recorded in his diary: 'The greatest error that ever our Island committed was the admitting of the Scottish Regiment'.

The First Civil War followed.

Carisbrooke Castle is less than five miles from Godshill Village. The surrender of the Castle by the step-father of the 2nd Baronet Worsley is mentioned in section 9.

More central to the nation's history was the sequence of events that led to the Castle becoming at first the refuge and then the prison of King Charles I, from November 1647 to September 1648. The general lack of sympathy on the Island with the royal cause was attributed by some to these earlier sufferings. After a period of fruitless negotiation in Newport (IoW), the King was taken as prisoner from the Island to imprisonment on the mainland, trial and within two months, execution.

ELEVEN
PERSONAL REMEMBERING - WILLS & GRAVESTONES

A Will today is a private document, only until it goes through the process called Probate, and public access to old wills is similarly available. Here we summarise a few.

William Legg of Stenbury Manor died 1581, Will proved 1583.
Tenant of John Worsley of Appuldurcombe, and also employee (probably Farm Manager). John Worsley, who died 1580, appointed William Legg one of his executors and left him a legacy and pension in gratitude for 'good advice and aid'.

He bequeathed to his wife Katharine £100 in ready money, all her wearing apparel, 1 feather bed & bolster, 2 pillows, a coverlet of yellow yarn, 2 pairs of sheets, a pair of blankets, a standing bedstead, and furniture in the chamber over the parlour. He also bequeathed to his son Thomas Legg the residue of the estate, after other bequests.

To other son Andrew (still a minor), £60.13.4d and the request that he continued in education.

The daughters: Ursula (no legacy), Elizabeth (£50) and Mary (£5)

The grandchildren (children of Mary & David Urry):

David, Thomas & Mary (each a yearling bullock, 6 lambs & £3).

His own brothers & sisters : Lewis, John, Alice Rokeley, Margaret Dore, Alice Bartlett (each 5/8d).

Richard Garde of Princelett wished his body to be buried in the entrance to the Church,

Henry Combes of Rowde (Will of 1619) also instructed similarly.

Richard Colman of Upper Appleford, Churchwarden, also asked to be buried in the Church. He made provision for the poor of four villages: 40/- to Godshill, 10/- to Whitwell (then within Godshill parish), 10/- to Niton and 10/- to Chale.

"Item, I give   to my daughter Ann Bull 20/-
                        to Thomas Bull ye elder of Mottistone a ewe sheep

Item, I give   to John Williams of Shorwell one sheep
                        to John Williams the younger, my nephew £20

Item, I give   to Eleanor Williams my niece £20

Item, I give   to Thomas Bull my nephew and Jane Bull my niece,
                        I give ten ewe sheep, apiece,
                        to my son John Colman I give all my remaining sheep
                        to my sons Launcelot Colman and John Colman
                                 I give all my bonds and my bills

Item, I give   to my son Launcelot Colman my tenements lying in the parish of
                        Gatcombe paying fourpence by the year to John Worsley Esq

All the rest   to my son Launcelot Colman my executor."

(The Testator does not include his sister, but only her husband John Williams and son.)

Richard Colman died in 1625 and this Will was proved at Winchester in 1629.

Richard Love of Little Stenbury Farm (Will of 1639)
His Will shows that he owned Love's Farm, later owned by Edward Legg (below). There are still 'Love's Cottages' in Sainham Lane.

Thomas Legg of Stenbury Manor (Will dated 1668)
"To John Legg, my son, ten ewes of our score sheep. I do give him the household stuffe and I give him the property of that tenement, and after his decease verile (verily) of that estate unto Edward Legg, his assigns and I do give him £50 in money. (Edward was John's younger brother)

Item, I give   unto Thomas Legg, my grandson, my son Thomas Legg's son,
                        £50 and to his two sisters £10 apiece,

Item, I give   unto Arthur Legg my grandson, ten years in my house, which
                        his mother do now dwell in Newport. [3]

Item, I do give   my daughter Mary Petis £20 and unto her husband £20 which I
                        lent him."[4]

(Edward later owned Saynham Farm & lands called 'Loves', Godshill. When he died in 1670, he left those properties to his son Thomas.)

1678 - Other information from the 17th Century is afforded by the Worsley Account Book.

A thatched cottage named 'Broomhill' at the foot of Gatcliff was let to John Legg. 'Mr Robert Harrison (the Vicar) paid for a year's Rent of Little Stenbury the sum of £12.' (Godshill had no Parsonage House, and he had to make his own arrangements. If this was a small farm, it was not unusual for a cleric to engage in farming, and those with glebe would often farm at least part of it themselves.)

---

[3] Does this mean "...as his mother now lives elsewhere"?

[4] That is, the debt is forgiven.

'Mr Legg for the year ending Lady Day, for Downe Place the sum of £10.'
'Mr Legg of Love's the sum of £1.' (Two different members of the Legg family.)
'William Reynolds for the rent of Itchalls the sum of £1.5.0d.'

Hatchments are the diamond-shaped paintings of arms, prepared for display on death, and often then hung in the Parish Church. Three of those in Godshill Church are predictably from Appuldurcombe: the 6th Baronet (with his wife's), the 7th Baronet (without his wife's) and Lord Yarborough. Another is from a Tollemache, 5th Earl of Dysart from Cheshire who died at Steephill Cove in 1821, within Godshill parish.

A substantial clearance of the Churchyard in 1923 brought into view a number of memorial stones previously obscured by growth. The churchyard contains several recumbent monoliths. The oldest is from the 14th century. The earliest dated one is to Richard (1593) and Anne (1592) Gard, the parents of the school benefactor (section 7).

One coffin-shaped stone was marked on one side 'R.G.1675' and on the other 'I.G.1669', and may relate to the Garde family. A similar stone (1615) has on one side 'W.S.' and on the other 'E.S'. Nearby were three similar coffin-shaped stones with no inscription, also 17th century. Near them was a stone bearing initials 'R.M.' with an open heart (to signify grief) and a lozenge (to signify widowhood), and another 'R.C. - 1670' with on the reverse an open heart, lozenge and two intersecting triangles with circle.

In the clearing of the Churchyard in 1923, two table-tombs were rescued from the vegetation and their inscriptions where possible deciphered. The older one was of Elizabeth Legge who died in the 17th century, who had come from Dorset, the wife of John Legge of Stenbury. The later had its inscription in copper and relates to Richard Legge, perhaps her son, who died in 1641.

Near the wall of the north transept was a large table-tomb of John Bushell (d. 1656). The lettering is 'Caroline miniscule' with many letters joined, and words separated by lozenges. As he died four years before the end of the incumbency of John Bushell, in the absence of some mistake with the Vicar's dates, he is thought to be the Vicar's son. There is word-play in the epitaph with repetition of the word 'blush', ending:
Death ne'er did blush this truth to testify
He did not blush to live nor did he blush to die.'

The Davis family is represented by a gravestone to John senior (d.1725) and his young daughter aged 15. His trade is celebrated with carvings of different carpenters' tools. He probably lived at Sainham. Again there is advice:
'God grant you all, who on us cast an eye
May straightway go and wisely learn to die.'

On the headstone to Nicholas Devenish (d.1730), among the carvings were two torches inverted, the symbolism of which is not clear. Nearby was one to Mary the wife of Gabriel Way, decorated with carvings of two hearts, joined together by thigh bones!

A memorial tablet, matching the floor inside, on the plain outside wall of the north transept is 'in memory of Thomas Allenstone, Mason, who died on October 28th 1743 aged 73 years.' He was the master mason who was responsible for re-building that part of the church, memorial to two Worsley brothers.

There are nine striking stones of the family of Bartholomew Jacobs, long established on the Island, and one branch of which lived in Godshill during the 18th century. There are cherubs' heads, drooping roses, trumpets and books for the recording angels. There are torches and lamps, garlands and an urn like a soup tureen. Robert Jacobs (d.1743) offers advice to those who visit his grave:

'Labour to keep a conscience pure
When all things fail, this will endure.'

Bartholomew Jacobs (d.1757) has as epitaph:

'Man is the seed, God is the sower
Man is grass, Death is the mower.'

Mary Jacobs (also died 1757) speaks from her resting place:

'Christian reader cast an eye
As you are now so once was I
As I am now so you must be
Prepare yourself to follow me.'

Another Bartholomew Jacobs (d.1768) son of the above after whom he was named, was buried nearby. He clearly left a widow and offspring for his epitaph bids her

'Weep not for me, but love the children.'

Martha (d. 1780) is assumed to be that wife, and she too bids those who visit her grave to cease from tears.

A stone originally marking the grave of George Abbot (d.1689) of Rowde had been re-used (palimsest). In addition to an hour-glass was a heart doubly pierced, which may well indicate two loves in his life. When lifted in 1923, on the reverse of the same stone were found two carefully engraved copper plates to Elizabeth Fallick (d.1765) and her husband William Fallick (d.1790). Her epitaph reads:

"Death takes the good, too good on earth to stay
And leaves the bad, too bad to take away.'

He paid certain rent to Magdalene ('Maudlins') College Oxford for permission to keep open a small chapel at Appleforde. His epitaph was:

'With patience to the last he did submit/
Nor murmured not at what the Lord thought fit.
He with a Christian courage did resign
His soul to God in his appointed time.'

One headstone commemorates the 19-year-old wife of John Loader, with new born twins who all died in 1775. It depicts the Book of Judgment. An arm emerging from thunderous clouds holds up a coffin-lid. An angel blows his trumpet and points to skeletons of the hapless trio. Contrasted with Death with his dart, is Christ the Saviour and to him

'all my friends that are behind
Will soon come after me.'

A plain headstone close to the wall marked the grave of John Bull (d.1790) aged 40 from Bagwich Farm whose family gave the land for the building of a Chapel.[5]

The wasting sickness or consumption was rampant (known to us as tuberculosis). A headstone was found of a girl of 18 named Jane Kingswell who died in 1809.

> 'A pale consumption struck the fatal blow
> The effect was certain but the time was slow
> With lingering pains Death saw me long oppressed
> Pitied my griefs and took me to my rest.'

Naval Captain William Grove died aged 58 at his house in Chale in 1822. We read:

> 'Through Neptune's waves of tempest toss't
> He ploughed for forty years
> Though thrice shipwrecked, but never lost
> Nor felt unmanly fears.
> Once did he 'scape a watery grave
> By floating on an oar
> When all the crew beneath the wave
> Went down to rise no more.
> But any means where God shall please
> To cut the mortal thread
> For he thus saved from raging seas
> Departed in his bed.

It is difficult not to smile.

Thomas Whitewood was leader of the first Methodists who gathered in Rookley, and he died in 1826. His epitaph praises his Christian generosity and attention to duty.

The last place of John Bagwell (d.1837) was marked with only a few words.

> 'Praises on stones are words but vainly spent
> A man's good name is his best monument.'

By the sundial there are grave-stones with expertly cut lettering, and acanthus & floral decoration. Elsewhere in the churchyard are representations of skulls and of cross-bones indicating one attitude to death, and cherubs to indicate another. There are also hour-glasses and obelisks under weeping willows.

There was in former times a real sense of unity and continuity between this world and the next, and thus of the living and the dead. In Godshill Churchyard generation after generation were buried, all sorts and conditions of men, women and children. Most graves were either unmarked or the marker (being of wood) long since perished.   Gravestones before 1660 were fairly rare, and for generations after then were for those who could afford them. Not until the 20th century did Godshill provide a burial site elsewhere than the yard surrounding the Church on the Knoll, with more spaces marked than unmarked.

---

[5] see Section K

K
NON-CONFORMITY from 1689

The Toleration Act (1689) enabled those dissenting from the ways of the Church of England, other than Roman Catholics and Unitarians, to form their own separate meetings. Many attended the Parish Church at Easter and Christmas to receive communion, and all were obliged to do so for weddings, baptisms if desired, and burial. These dissenting groups were particularly strong among trades-people, artisans and craftsmen and among the labouring classes. Thus it was the well-to-do and those whom they influenced such as their servants who stayed with the Church of England, but the former were not as regular in attendance as were the dissenters.

Non-conformists were increasing in number in Godshill parish, and they built a 'weatherboard' Chapel on a site opposite the present Primary School. Much of the timber was salvaged from ships wrecked off the south coast of the Island. The land was given by Farmer John Bull of Bagwich Manor, who died that same year of 1790. An account of his gravestone, quotes his epitaph, visible in 1946 but since obscured:

'Pain was my portion, physic was my food,
Groans my devotion, drugs did me no good
But Christ the physician, knowing what was best
To ease me of my pains, he took my soul to rest.'

The Bull family had given hospitality to visiting missionary preachers from the mainland for the previous two decades. The Chapel opening ceremony in 1790 was conducted by Jasper Winscom, a Wesleyan Minister sent as missionary to the Island by John Wesley.

The relationship between Anglicans and those who dissented depended largely on the attitude of their leaders, and in the time of the Rev Henry Worsley was tolerant and cordial.

It was not long before the Godshill Methodist congregation was ready to build a larger and somewhat grander chapel. Lord Yarborough gave them a piece of land at the Shanklin end of the High Street on which they built the present Chapel, and indeed assisted them further financially.

In the 1830s in the Godshill area were other thriving Non-conformist congregations. At Sandford, Roud and Rookley, all within the ecclesiastical parish of Godshill, groups of dissenting Christians had grown into congregations, and permanent buildings for their worship were erected. However, the School was firmly Anglican both in teaching and in general culture. It was overseen by the Vestry of the parish church. This was a further source of grievance to be borne by the non-conformist families until they could arrange their own type of school within reasonable distance, and indeed agree between them sufficiently to support a new foundation. This was a transitional time between there being a single acknowledged and legal Church (the Church of England) and full legal and social capacity to worship as one chose, with corresponding equality of social status for Non-conformists.

TWELVE
APPULDURCOMBE FROM 1768

Richard Worsley's father died in 1768 when the future 7th Baronet was 17. After Winchester, he went to Corpus Christi College Oxford, but appears not to have graduated. Instead, he embarked on a two-year Grand Tour of the continent with a Swiss tutor recommended by Gibbon, one George Deyverdan. At Oxford he was described by Edward Gibbon as a 'wild English buck', 'a dashing fellow' and 'a gambler, dandyish and gay in his behaviour'. The tour changed him greatly, and Gibbon commented that the 21-year-old Richard had 'grown into a philosopher' who 'hardly ever smiled and never laughed'. He was given to quoting Montaigne the French 16th century moralist, and to drinking only water. He boasted of his ability to exercise control over all bodily passions.

Sir Richard had a fierce desire to raise the standing of the family on the Island to its earlier level, and his marriage in 1775 formed part of that plan. His bride was both beautiful and rich, Seymour Dorothy Fleming from Middlesex & Huntingdonshire. Edward Gibbon commented that his friend may have married for love 'but he also married for a sum of £80,000'. Two children were born, but both died in early life.

Sir Richard dedicated himself to completing two unfinished works begun by his predecessors: the building of Appuldurcombe House, and the compiling of the History of the Isle of Wight. Work on the building resumed in 1772, with some amendment to the design. The names of James Wyatt and Thomas Chippendale are both mentioned as designers, probably of the interior and furniture. The baronet also commissioned the popular landscape designer "Capability" Brown to re-design the grounds in the style then fashionable, including a sham Gothic folly built on St Martin's Down, which came to be known as "Cook's Castle' - since destroyed. An Obelisk was erected of Cornish granite, but a lightning strike in 1831 reduced this to a sorry state. A fine triumphal arch in the Ionic style was set up as entrance on the Godshill side: the Freemantle Gate.

Management of the works was in the hands of William Donn, who was paid between the years 1774 and 1782 sums totalling £4,000, with some others paid separately including James Wyatt, 'Capability' Brown, and Mr Vangilden the supplier of decorative chimney pieces. The whole enterprise was completed in or soon after 1782.

The most widely admired part of the exterior has been the east facade, facing St Martin's Down, and that was begun and almost certainly completed to the original design of 1701. Shortage of funds forced Sir Richard into economies, which led one critic to write that the house 'stands like a mushroom in the open lawn'. Another commented that the 'architecture cannot be commended' an opinion probably resulting from the changes in design during the century. Sir Richard himself considered that his considerable additions much improved on the original design.

The finished house had all four elevations in Corinthian style in free-stone with detailed features in Portland stone, under a roof of Westmorland slates. The entrance hall was 54 feet long and 24 feet wide, with eight Ionic columns. On the first and attic floors were upwards of twenty bed-chambers with dressing rooms.

While the work was proceeding, his Mother and young sister were living with the 7th Baronet, and visitors were received in appropriate style and much music-making, including Edward Gibbon and the radical politician & journalist John Wilkes. It was in 1772 that Wilkes secured an invitation to Appuldurcombe, through his host Captain Bissett of Knighton Gorges Manor (Newchurch, IoW). Wilkes was impressed by the 'grand breakfast and the musical gifts of the Worsleys'.

Sir Richard followed his predecessors in being given Royal offices. From 1777 he was appointed to the group which transacted the King's household financial business. He was sworn in as a Privy Councillor, and became Member of Parliament for a 'Rotten Borough' on the Island, where he became Governor of the Isle of Wight. At this point, all seemed set fair for the reputation of the 7th Baronet. His influence was substantial. In addition to the Manors of Godshill and Appuldurcombe, he held the Manors of Chale, Chessell, Shalfleet, St Lawrence, Stenbury, Whitwell, La Wode Middleton & Wolverton otherwise Bembridge, Week & Sandford, and Apse, (but had disposed of Gatcombe to the Worsley living there). In a list of rents in the Island payable to the Crown in 1780, his name appears three times: as paying for Roud, Rew and Middleton, for the Manor of Apse, and for both the Manor and the Rectory of Godshill.

John Wilkes continued to cultivate the acquaintance of the Worsleys and to visit Appuldurcombe. It is not known whether Sir Richard and Lady Seymour were aware that he was at the same time a prominent member of what was popularly known as the Hell Fire Club at Medmenham near Henley-on-Thames. Their meetings were noted for riotous living and sexual laxity. It is known that Wilkes tried to recruit to this notorious club his associates at house parties at Knighton Gorges, the Island home of Captain Bissett around 1780. Other well-known visitors there were Joshua Reynolds (Portrait Painter) and David Garrick (Actor - Manager).

By this time the lack of moral rectitude of Lady Seymour Worsley became apparent, and she began to bestow her favours on house guests including Lord Dearcroft, Lord Peterborough and the Marquis of Grantham. It appears that Captain Bisset was led by the influence of Wilkes into fascination with the aristocratic circle, and not only visited Appuldurcombe but also was a member of the Worsleys' party on visits elsewhere. There is some evidence that Sir Richard encouraged a liaison between Lady Seymour and Capt Bissett, provided it remained a private matter within their circle. This was naive, and the adulterous relationship became in 1781 an elopement at the mercy of common gossip. The reaction of Sir Richard to the public nature of the relationship was to sue Captain Bissett for a large sum in damages. At that time, an action could lie on grounds of 'criminal conversation'. The assumption was that the man took the initiative in alienating the affections of a passive and innocent wife, which did not seem to square with the facts.

The case attracted much attention when it came on before Lord Mansfield. For the prosecution, waiters and chambermaids from the Royal Hotel in Pall Mall gave evidence as to the couple's stay in Room 14. Captain Bissett's defence was robust. Its first leg was that the lady was far from innocent. His Counsel accused her of having sexual relationships with thirty-four partners, which she denied, but she subsequently admitted twenty seven, many of them of the nobility. The second leg of his case was that Sir Richard had actively encouraged his wife's behaviour.

Sir Richard had claimed £20,000. He was granted one shilling. The lower end of the national Press made much of the case, and all three of the principals were the subject of caricature and ridicule. Sir Richard did try to take advantage of the situation to purchase the Knighton Gorges Estate from Capt Bissett but was rebuffed.

Lady Seymour discontinued use of the name Worsley, and lived in isolation, the victim of venereal disease. It was subsequently suggested that her syphilitic condition accounted for the absence of a living heir to her husband's estate.

Sir Richard's reaction to the situation was to travel abroad extensively in southern Europe and beyond, from 1783 to 1787. He indulged his taste in antiques with advantageous purchases. So numerous were his art acquisitions that Sir Richard hired a ship to transport them back to England to stock Appuldurcombe House. On his return he continued final improvements to the house, gardens and park. Now however he was not creating a family home, but a museum of fine arts. One famous antiquarian, described the house as having 'an air of melancholy and magnificence.' The human soul had given place to that melancholic collection. In 1793 he became the King's representative in Venice, and was engaged in reporting the movement of Napoleon's armies until that Republic fell to the French.

In 1798 and 1803 Sir Richard published two volumes of engraved copies of many of his artistic treasures, whilst himself living in seclusion much of the time at a cottage that he had built in Luccombe and at Marine Villa in St Lawrence. He was looked after by a lady whom he called his housekeeper, Mrs Sarah Smith. Sir Richard died childless in 1805, aged 54, and within a month his widow re-married.

It was his niece who succeeded to the estate (but not of course to the baronetcy), and it was she who commissioned for Godshill Church a massive monumental sarcophagus in memory of Sir Richard. It was originally sited in the south transept, earlier St Stephen's Chapel, but latterly has been re-sited at the west end behind the organ. Village people have dubbed it 'the Tub'. An example of Sir Richard's art collection is hung on the north wall: 'Daniel in the Lions' Den, earlier thought to be a Rubens. There is also a hatchment with his armorial bearings.

Sir Richard's niece married Charles Anderson Pelham who became Lord Yarborough of Brocklesby Park in Lincolnshire, which was their mainland seat. They used Appuldurcombe house only as a summer residence, but she died in 1813. The close relationship which had endured for 283 years between the Worsleys and the village of Godshill now came to an end. The Worsley name was associated with Appuldurcombe only by the title Baron Worsley given to Lord

Yarborough. He was First Commodore of the Royal Yacht Squadron stationed at Cowes (IoW). He erected a Semaphore apparatus near the Obelisk to communicate most swiftly with the coast. This aspect of his life became sufficiently important that he made improvements to Appuldurcombe House. He also involved himself in the affairs of the village including the School, Vestry meetings, and the building of the Griffin Inn. He gave the local Methodist congregation a piece of land at the Shanklin end of the High Street on which they built the present Chapel.

As he grew older, however, Lord Yarborough was less and less on the Island. The less important works of art were the subject of gift locally, and All Saints Church Godshill was among the beneficiaries. Other items and furniture were taken to Lincolnshire, and others again were transported to the British Museum for display. He died in 1846 and after a while arrangements were made to sell the Appuldurcombe Estate. The house became an empty shell, and was never again to be lived in as a family home.

In 1859 a purchaser was found, but plans for conversion to a Hotel never came to fruition. [6] In 1867, the property was leased to the Revd Mr Pound for use as a College for Young Gentlemen, which did have the merit of providing some employment for village people. In precarious circumstances this use ceased in 1901, which by chance was the year Queen Victoria died at Osborne House (IoW).

The first modest house back in Norman times had been a monastic establishment, and there was a certain aptness in the next use. A band of Benedictine Monks from Solesmes in France had plans to build a new Monastery on the site of the old and long-since ruined Quarr Abbey. They needed temporary accommodation, and took a lease of Appuldurcombe. They lived and worshipped in the Godshill area from 1901 to 1908, whilst designing and building the red-brick Abbey on the site of the medieval monastery at Quarr.

Six years later, the empty house was again put to temporary use, as a military hospital and rehabilitation centre. From 1918 to 1939 the house again stood unoccupied and the fabric deteriorated. In 1932, after a visit to the Island, Queen Mary was associated with attempts to save the house as of national heritage

---

[6] A magnificent mausoleum, built to contain a small dynasty, can be found on the Eastern edge of the graveyard. It contains an adult lead coffin, a baby's lead coffin, and an ash-urn. Due to lack of maintenance by the family it became derelict, and many attempts were made to steal the lead coffins, which have now been bricked in under the bottom shelf. It must be presumed that Robert's second (and much younger) wife, once she remarried, felt no sense of obligation to the family from whom she had inherited. The plaques on the mausoleum read:

Robert Vaughan Wynne Williams Esq. of Appuldurcombe. Born 26.10.1798, died 1.6.1862. (Bur. 6.6.1862)'

Heriot Jones Wynne Williams, infant son of above born 5 Aug 1862 died 6 Nov 1862. (Bur. 11.11.1862)

and

Sydney Rebecca Louisa Williams, daughter of Robert Vaughan Wynne Williams, who died in Switzerland, 30.6.1836

importance, but the Second World War intervened. Again the house served the need for a Military Hospital, on this occasion for wounded officers. A land-mine dropped by the Luftwaffe caused extensive damage in 1943, which led to the building being evacuated. At the end of the war the most likely fate was total demolition for reasons of safety. A writer in 'Country Life' in the 1950s considered that 'this magnificent Queen Anne House was worthy of proposals to preserve its architectural features for posterity'. The suggestion was that it be moved stone by stone to a war-damaged city for re-erection. This did not happen, but those in authority were persuaded that this Classical Palladian ruin of a once stately and historic home should be placed in the care of the Ministry of Public Buildings and Works. It was acknowledged to be part of our national heritage.

L
THE 1820s

If the Vestry, the only organ of Local Government, did in fact fail to meet for ten years prior to 1829, this may link with the general malaise of those years. The long and costly Napoleonic Wars had left a bitter aftermath of agricultural depression, monetary inflation and unemployment. Poor harvests had made an immediate impact. The increasing use of new methods in agriculture, however efficient, in the short term meant lack of work on the farms especially during the winter. It is this seasonal difficulty which accounts for the frustration and anger being focussed on the new threshing machines. Non-conformity was growing apace in Godshill, with understandable criticism of the Vestry form of government which was so closely Anglican in origin. Moreover there were strong stirrings towards more democratic forms, and the Vestry was in no sense a democratically constituted body. The workings of the Vestry were put under scrutiny by those who were excluded, whether by religious dissent or social standing. The repeal of the Test and Corporation Acts (1828) enabled both Dissenters and Roman Catholics to take public office.

It may also be significant that the apparent collapse of the vestry system in Godshill coincided with the last years of the Revd John Barwis. He had come into the incumbency in 1786, and did not retire from it until 42 years later in 1828. He lived throughout in Niton. It is understood that he retired to Cumberland. It seems likely that his successor, the Revd Richard Dixon, although similarly living out of Godshill and employing a Curate for Godshill, would provide the initiative for the re-calling of the Vestry, and the keeping of minutes of the business transacted. A general tightening of business matters and procedures is to be expected on the arrival of a new man.

This was a time when low wages and high prices had led to many parishes using the poor rate to supplement the wages of those in employment, a step taken originally from humanitarian motives but which had dire results in keeping wages low. A farm labourer's weekly wage might be less than 15 shillings a week, but a 4lb loaf of bread cost one-twelfth of that, fluctuating in price according to the local harvest.

***

By contrast, the 1830s was a decade of reforms, and the growing realisation that efficient local government rested on efficient administration. Although the mighty swings of national and indeed international economic cycles were not susceptible to administrative control, the rest of the 19th century was marked by more and more decisions being taken out of the hands of residents of small communities such as Godshill, to distant centres of power.

THIRTEEN
19th CENTURY CHARITIES & SCHOOL

In 1835, in the middle of an active reforming decade nationally, the Crown Commissioners put in hand an enquiry into the Charities associated with several parishes on the Isle of Wight, including Godshill. The resulting Report was the first instalment of a record which they asked should be preserved and studied, so that local people might be more aware what charities existed. That would be likely to ensure proper administration into the future with accounts produced at the annual Vestry at Easter. Other reports followed later in the century.

Their judgment in 1835 on past administration was clear. 'The information we are about to publish will, we (the Commissioners) believe to be interesting and valuable, and such as has not hitherto been within the reach of the general reader. In past times there can be no doubt that charities disappeared from view, being swallowed up by men who were able to cloak their misdeeds in the midst of ignorance, which hung so thickly over the land.'

Richard Gard of Princelett had in his Will of 1617 made a gift not only to the school (see section 7) but also separately for the poor of parishes including Godshill. In the second quarter of the 19th century this was being duly paid by John White, then owner of the estate at Brading on which it had been originally charged known formerly as 'Blackpan' but then as 'Merry Gardens'. The custom had been for the Churchwardens to pay small sums out in cash, but it was in 1837 proposed to add to the Communion Alms the sum recently received in order to purchase coals for distribution to the needy in Godshill. The Gard bequest was distributed in 1873(????) in the form of bread.

Sir Richard Worsley had in the early 16th century created an annuity of £10 a year for the benefit of 8 poor widows of Godshill, in addition to his gift for the school (see section 7). It was still being paid in 1825, but there was little continuity in the records. It had for many years been paid to the Worsley Almshouses in Newport (IoW). Both the school and the poor annual gifts were charged on the Manors of Chale and Walpen. Lord Yarborough sold that property in 1806, but it was overlooked that the property was so burdened, and Lord Yarborough continued making the payments, of which the Purchaser had been ignorant. The payments were still being made in 1892 (further Report). School annuities included one from 1604 given by Philip Andrews, and that too was being paid in 1892, by James Harvey the owner of Marvel farm, just south of Newport. The Free Grammar School had charitable income of £33, and there was also a mid-Victorian benefactor to the poor named Dixon.

An earlier benefactress who lived in the parish was a widow, probably of the Meux family, named Elizabeth Duncannson. She lived in the first quarter of the 18th century and had nearly a dozen pieces of land on the Rookley side of Godshill village at Leak. She also had leaseholds, one occupied by one Calloway, and also 'Cooks' which she had received from the Meux estate when that family name became extinct for want of a male heir. Some of her benefactions (to benefit 6 widows, 6 poor children and a Mission in Newport) were by her Will to cease after 20 years. Other gifts were in perpetuity: towards building places of worship and to make grants to missionaries. The identity of her Trustees makes it clear that she was a member of the Congregational dissenting sect.

Summary of other C17th Donors:

William Dale, farmer near Bathingbourne	annuity	£5
- Farr, farmer		£5
William Oglander		10/-
William Thatcher		10/-

***

The Revd Henry Worsley first signed Vestry Minutes as Minister in 1813. He was related to the Appuldurcombe family, but of the branch of the family whose seat was at Gatcombe. He was Curate of Godshill under the non-resident Vicar, who held the two livings of Godshill and Niton and lived at Niton. Mr Worsley also held the post of Master of the Grammar School. The taking of two such incomes was quite usual.

Mr Worsley was popular in his capacity as Curate of Godshill. He was regarded as handling sensitively the difficult relations with non-conformists. At this time they were compelled to call upon the services of the Church of England for making their communion, for weddings and for funerals. However in his capacity as Master, he was not successful in attracting scholars in the classics. Notwithstanding the low school roll, he drew his salary from the School trust as well as from the Church. In other words the Grammar School existed as a legal entity, but scarcely in practice.

The 'blending' of the two boys' schools may seem obvious to us and a positive step, but it was in fact in breach of the terms of the Grammar School trusts. It was either in ignorance or defiance of the Lord Chancellor's ruling in 1805 that it amounted to mis-application of Grammar School trust funds to teach any subject other than the Classics and English including some literature. It was not until 1840 that Parliament gave to the authorities of endowed schools the legal power to widen the scope of the terms under which endowments had been made, if the Trustees so wished. In doing so Parliament was ratifying a widespread practice. Long after the event, we may consider that this anticipation in Godshill of the subsequent relaxing of that decision was for the greater good.

In 1836, it was unanimously resolved in Public Meeting that Thomas Finnemore, who had served for twenty years, 'be removed, a month from this day, from the situation of the Free School and Gard Ushership and put on his retirement from the school.' Although he was given £10 by the parish, there appears to have been general dissatisfaction at the conduct of the school, not only in size of roll, but also in teaching and discipline.

In 1837, an official Report on the school was made. It records : 'Mr Worsley informs us that until 5 or 6 years before his appointment a Classical School was maintained by his predecessor, John Lancaster 1806-1807, and was accommodated in the Old Chantry House, both for boarders and for day scholars'. He further states 'that he, himself, first took day scholars when he was appointed with an assistant Usher, to teach them writing and Arithmetic, together with Classics, but, finding that there was no sufficient numbers of scholars to support his plan, he established a 'Day School' under his assistant, the children to be taught *in his assistant's house* (editor's italics).   This accommodation was for those children who did not object to being taught by the Usher, and reserving to Mr Worsley (the Master) the day scholars who were to be taught Classics at a charge of 3 guineas per quarter.' (The word 'free' seems to have been over-looked.) Mr Worsley further reported 'that he had not received any such day - scholars, but that he was still ready to receive both boys and girls under his arrangements.' The Usher's wife had discontinued teaching after two years. There is no mention of the School building erected only 15 years before, which was perhaps outside the scope of the Report.

On Thomas Finnemore's departure, William Read was appointed to both 'the Free School & Guard Ushership'. At the 1837 Vestry he was re-appointed, and this was now an annual appointment, but the designation of 'Usher' was replaced by that of 'Schoolmaster'. In 1838 William Read was re-appointed Schoolmaster 'for the year next ensuing' along with the Church Sexton and the Vestry Clerk, and his social status may have been little higher than theirs.

It was in 1833 that Parliament voted the first small Grants towards the cost of educating the children of the country, after it was disclosed that no more than one-quarter of the children received any form of education. One was to the (Anglican) National Society. Godshill was able to obtain a grant from the National Society, since the terms of the endowments at Godshill placed the school under the aegis

of the Church of England. This was a time nationally of rivalry betwee
established Church and Non-conformists, and this was particularly marke
relation to education. The source of the national grant sharpened the issue,
there began a shifting of emphasis and of power which has continued to this da

Lord Yarborough had been instrumental in the building of the Griffin Hote
mistakenly thinking it to be the heraldic beast of the Worsley family.[7] The 183
Vestry Meeting was held for the first time 'at the Vestry Room' there. For two years
(1837 & 1838) no clergyman signed the Minutes, but when the next year the
meeting was in the Parish Church again, the Minister (William John Hurnall)
signed.

The 1870 Act made elementary schooling compulsory. Godshill School was
inspected and deemed to be efficient. More accommodation was however
necessary to meet the larger school roll, and in 1881 the School buildings were
extended with the aid of a Government Grant. School Boards took over
management under central control, and in Godshill the influence of the Trustees,
the Vestry and the Vicar all diminished. Children with the potential for selection for
further education at Grammar School were throughout the country starting school
life alongside those with none.

In 1905, the School was leased at a small payment to the local Education
Committee, to take children of the locality from 5 to 14. Later, older children went
out of the village for Grammar School and Secondary School education.

---

[7] which in reality is the Wyvern

...shire,
...nne the heiress daughter of Sir John Leigh.
...)38
...as knighted by Henry VIII, & became Captain of the Island.
...extended the lease of Appuldurcombe.
...nne re-founded school.

RICHARD
Captain of the Island after father (except during Mary's reign).
Died 1565
Active in defence plans under Henry VIII.
In charge of sale of Church silver etc in reign of Edward VI. His sons died in an explosion.

JOHN
Succeeded brother, but had unsuccessful contest with Richard's widow's second husband for part of the property. Died 1580

THOMAS Only son of John

RICHARD
Son of Thomas, succeeded at age 15, lost an eye while hunting.
Died 1621
Was knighted and in 1611 became 1st Baronet, MP for Newport.
Boisterous.   Died after smallpox. Widow married Col. Brett

HENRY 2nd Baronet -
MP for Newport, & later Newtown, Involved for Parliament in Island Militia.
45 years as baronet.
Died 1666

ROBERT
3rd baronet - MP for Newtown.
Man of learning, keen traveller on the Continent.
Died 1676. At death son aged 7- guardian his uncle James,

ROBERT
4th Baronet - came of age in 1690. Later MP for Newport.
Died 1713
Started to re-build Appuldurcombe. Keener on garden. Lack of funds.
Died childless, succeeded by cousin.

JAMES
5th Baronet - learned antiquarian - lived in Hampshire -
started to collect material for History of Island - 43 years as baronet.
Died 1756

THOMAS
6th Baronet - keen Captain of South Hampshire Militia
Did not live permanently at Appuldurcombe.
At his death son was 17.
Died 1768

RICHARD
7th Baronet - continental tour - 1781 published History
Re-started building House till about 1782
MP & Governor of Island
1781 wife eloped with Bisset -infamous Court case.
1783 onwards much on the Continent collecting art treasures
Appuldurcombe became 'museum'.
Son Robert died, he died childless, 1805 & neice succeeded.

CHARLES
Husband of that neice became the 1st Earl of Yarborough,
Baron Worsley of Appuldurcombe.
At Appuldurcombe only in summer for Cowes yachting season,
1855 house put up for sale - never again family home.

FOURTEEN
GODSHILL GOVERNMENT: 1795 to 1840

In 1795 a History of the Isle of Wight was published by John Albin, written in the form of a travelogue from his journey accompanying the Marchioness of Clanricarde and her entourage. It was only a few years after the authoritative History of the Island written by Sir Richard Worsley, but it serves to give a different view.

John Albin predictably described the principal village as adjoining the Church and as consisting 'entirely of thatched cottages, having gardens annexed to them, with the Church on a natural pyramid in the centre exhibiting a very neat rustic picture'.

In the village itself there were some twelve such cottages on the north side of the High Street, eight on the south, and five around the Church entrance. In visiting Godshill Church, John Albin observes that several brasses were missing from memorial stones (including de Aula, de Heyno & Fry) 'probably stripped off in the Civil War period'.

Godshill's physical qualities in 1795: the land largely under the
' parts particularly suitable for raising 'forward lambs'. Harvest
⌐ than in other parts of the Island. The fields were mostly
⌐l-banks on which 'the underwood (made) good fences' - the word
what we would call a hedge. The parish was well provided with
⌐ coppices' and the whole was 'tolerably well wooded'. 'Only a very
⌐on of the land was waste.' By the standards of the day road surfaces
⌐ a red binding-gravel . . . (were) in most places pretty good'.   Before the
permanent surfaces to which we are accustomed, all highways were mere
⌐-tracks at the mercy of the weather, and relied on the ability of the Parish
⌐fficers to secure repair from local resources.

***

One record from 1796 is a written memorandum between the Revd John Barwis
and the occupiers of all the land in the parish. They agreed to commute the Vicar's
tithes payable in kind into an annual cash sum (£106.7s.6d), the burden of which
they would then apportion between the parishioners.   Private compositions of this
nature were frequently made in the 18th century, before the Tithe Act of 1836
made commutation compulsory.

The only Local Government at parish level at the end of the 18th century was the
body called the Vestry, responsible historically for Church matters.

There is some indication that in 1806 the Vestry were making fresh efforts to
collect the charitable moneys due. (It may of course be that earlier records have
not been preserved.)   We know that the annual sum given by Richard Gard in
the early 17th century for the Poor of Godshill was paid due at Christmas 1805, by
the then owner of Blackpan Farm John White esq. Similarly recorded are
payments made out of the income on Bathingbourne, Princelett and West
Nunwell.

Music in Church was at that time generally led by instrumentalists and singers
from a Gallery, usually at the west end. Pipe Organs had not often featured earlier
in village churches, but were coming into fashion. The 'Singing Gallery' at Godshill
was in the south side of the double nave. In 1813, Godshill Vestry resolved in
principle to install an organ. A year passed, during which the necessary
permission (a Faculty) from the Bishop's office was obtained. Formal Notice was
then given in terms which were probably provided from the Bishop's legal office:
>'The Ministers and Churchwardens of this Parish hereby call a Vestry
>to be holden in this church on Thursday 1st day of December next
>at 3 of the clock in the afternoon precisely that the said Churchwardens
>may then and there receive instructions for making a fair and
>proportionate Church Rate on all and everyone of the inhabitants
>of the Parish for the purpose of defraying all expenses incurred
>by purchasing and erecting an Organ in the Gallery at the west end
>of the Church.'
The faculty was to be exhibited at the Vestry meeting.

There was a proposal to erect an additional gallery, at the west end on the north
side. It was intended 'for the accommodation of the increased (number of) Poor',

which one takes to mean their segregation from the respectable. Nothing c
it.

There are no surviving Minutes between February 1819 and 1829. This w
time nationally for attempts at making Vestry membership more democratic,
regulating their business. The record from June 1829 reads: 'No vestry is le
unless three days notice thereof is given and published in Church on a Sunday.
Chairman must be appointed who shall have a casting vote. Every perso
assessed of less than £50 to have one vote. Persons assessed at £50 and
upwards shall have one vote for every £25 of their assessment, but not to exceed
6 votes to the same person.'

In 1830 the Vestry was dealing with the appointment of James Griffiths as Sexton
at an annual salary of £5, payable half yearly. He was to be responsible for
'sweeping the Church, washing the linen, fetching the Sacrament bread and wine,
and for drawing up the clock' (activated by gravity lowering its weight down the
inside of the tower over probably 24 hours). James Griffiths took the precaution of
adding to the Minute a note that 'oyl and Cleaning the Clock always excepted'.
These duties were additional to the care of the churchyard and gravedigging,
presumably too well-known to be specified.

There was a great deal of business connected with the relief of the poor of the
parish. Years before, in 1770, the gentlemen of the Island had been concerned at
the level of poverty and (more cynically one suggests) the rising level of Rates to
meet the costs of Parish Workhouses. All over the country in rural areas it was
being discovered that it was financially more effective to have a combined
arrangement for a group of parishes. This required an Act of Parliament, and in
1771 the Island Act which these gentlemen initiated was duly passed. The
Godshill Workhouse at the top end of 'Poor House Shute' serving the one parish
was replaced by a shared Island House of Industry erected for the purpose in
Parkhurst Forest.

The Preamble to the Act was largely worded in standard if optimistic form. It was
held that the providing of a House of Industry for the general reception of the Poor
would be more effective in several categories of inmate: in giving relief of the aged
infirm and diseased who proved incapable of supporting themselves, in employing
the able-bodied industrious, in correcting and punishing the idle, and in educating
the children of the destitute in both religion and work. The Poor would be enabled
to contribute to their own support, and thus less of a burden would fall on their
neighbours.

Within sixty years the economic situation nationally had further deteriorated and a
Parliamentary Commission was set up to investigate and report, after requesting
parishes to submit their findings. Godshill agreed that the 1601 Act was no longer
working well, and that, as the Guardians local arrangements had failed to improve
the situation, amendments to that Act were needed. Godshill favoured keeping the
House of Industry for the maintenance of indoor poor. The cost of the
establishment itself and its officers should be met by a general and equal rate. In
addition, each parish should be charged with the employment or relief of its own

...n their legal settlement. Rates should be paid by the proprietors ...eeding an annual value of £20, including lands owned by ...the parish. Emigration of Mechanics and others should be ...j rates.

...pal Poor Law Amendment Act and an Isle of Wight Act followed in ...while, in November 1833 Robert Buckett offered the Parish Officers to ...work at 8 shillings an acre for unemployed labourers to dig 10 acres of ...e offer of this employment was accepted.

...35, the Vestry wanted Joseph Tucker to be appointed Clerk 'in the room of ...j father recently deceased.' William Tucker had been Clerk from 1799 to 1832, ...when he was succeeded by James Griffin, the son of a former Churchwarden. The duties included not only book-keeping, Minute-taking and preparing and posting Notices of Meetings in due time, but also supervising the work of the Sexton.

In 1835 the Board of Guardians of the Poor relating to the whole Island were considering strategic matters on the working of the new Act. Should the total cost be spread across the Island, or should each parish be treated as a separate unit? With regard to the principle of settlement (the 'home' parish which was responsible for each poor person), should the unit be the whole Island, or should the parish boundaries be the deciding factor? Their Secretary wrote to each parish for an opinion. Godshill Vestry was unanimous that in both respects the Island should be treated as the unit.

It required a further Act of Parliament to replace the Isle of Wight House of Industry Act 1834. In 1837, the Vestry in considering the draft Bill, argued that the changes in population and the value of property since 1834 called for a corresponding change in the assessment of their parish. It consented to the repeal of the 1834 Isle of Wight Act in principle, and the Island being declared for rating and settlement purposes a single unit. It wanted the number of Poor Law Guardians raised from 5 to 15.

There was a further series of questions on Poor Law administration for the Vestry two months later. It was a cumbersome method to meet the growing demand for democracy at a time when central Government was starting to take more administrative powers. More legislation nationally in the 1830s meant more business for Godshill Vestry. The Vestry was still the agency of parish government despite its Anglican Church nature.

Godshill was now spreading the load of Poor Law business between four Overseers. It was also at this time that the Vestry were finding it wise to have their Solicitor Mr Thomas Sewell (see section 15) attend appropriate meetings. New valuations were needed, and a professional valuer was retained. The Clergy were sometimes absent from such meetings, but the Earl of Yarborough attended a meeting in November 1837, no doubt a reflection of the greater impact on his own finances at Appuldurcombe which the work of the Vestry was now having. Other landowners attending were Richard Harvey of Appleford, Daniel Attril (Farmer), Richard Cheverton of Lavenders Farm, William Hollis of Holden Farm, John Hollis of Orchards Farm, George White of Span Farm, William Griffin of Pond and T W Hardley (Landowner). April 1838 was the first meeting reco having met in the newly erected Griffin Hotel.

Vestry Meetings did of course also grapple with internal church matters, a November 1839 the conduct of the organist was under discussion, leading unanimous decision that he should continue in his situation till Easter with hope and expectation that his future conduct would meet with the approbation the Parishioners.

Among the business on the Agenda at the Annual General Meeting in 1840 was a call for ten employers to take apprentices by turn from the local House of Industry, and the list was completed at the meeting. The rest of the business was standard: examining and passing the Accounts of the Churchwardens and Overseers, agreeing the rate in the pound, the appointment of Vicar's Warden and Peoples' Warden, the appointment of the salaried officers for the ensuing year (Clerks, Sexton, Overseers). The Meeting was chaired by the Vicar's Warden, who duly signed the Book.

There was conflict between the Board of Guardians of the Poor and Godshill Vestry in 1840. Godshill had not agreed the original figures levied on the parish.

The response of the Guardians was to request the Vestry to form a Committee 'for the purpose of correcting any error that might have been made in the recent (rate) assessments'. The Vestry still considered that the Guardians demands had been 'unequal and unjust' (ie too heavy on Godshill rate-payers). Shortly afterwards the Vestry was forming a Committee 'to assist the Parish Officers in examining the new Rate Assessment.' This Committee of seven farmers made recommendations after several meetings: that assessments should be reduced on land (including buildings) by 15%, and on all other buildings by 20%, and that one-fourth of the Poor Rate be taken from certain tithes. There was to be provision for appeal, and five such appeals were later allowed. The rate for the quarter from Midsummer 1840 based on these revised assessments was voted through at 11 shillings in the pound. It is suggested that this episode shows how the power of the Vestry had been much reduced by the Poor Law Amendment Act of 1834. Funding the Houses of Industry and other Poor Relief absorbed a substantial proportion of the rates paid by parishioners, but control of many aspects had passed outside the parish.

.ople of every generation to suppose that they are the first to
.blems arising out of change. A moment's reflection tells us that
.ys with us.

.mer in the 19th century, there was constant pressure to adopt new
.: a steady procession of new machines were being produced, with
.ents patented and demonstrated at Agricultural Shows. Academics were
.ing for different means of improving the soil. Factories and importers were
.vertising the latest fertilizers or feed for livestock. Stock-breeding was under
constant discussion. In all these aspects, the larger landowner might be able to
afford to experiment, but the smaller farmer was essentially conservative and
cautious. Godshill farmers were slow to react in favour of 'new-fangled' ways.
While labour was cheap and plentiful, moreover, the local estate manager had
little incentive to be more productive as it meant throwing local men out of work.

One trend, as land-owning became less rewarding both financially and indeed in
the social scale, was the splitting up of larger estates. In the Godshill area, when
the opportunity arose, small farms of 30 to 50 acres were sold off. Six or eight
tenanted farms became owner-occupied, and the social mix of the parish changed
sharply when Appuldurcombe House ceased to be a family home.

Despite the arrival of steam traction engines for ploughing, the horse and
horseman retained a central place. However, where once a horseman might have
traced several generations working on the same estate in the same role, now the
changing of jobs and moving to an employer offering a better cottage became the
norm each Michaelmas.

***

Independence of spirit in employment matters was the counterpart perhaps of
independence of religious practice. The spread of Non-conformist beliefs may well
have included a readiness to challenge old practices. Gatherings of like-minded
folk in Christian worship led on to the forming of congregations needing their own
chapel building. In addition to the Primitive Methodist Chapel in the village of
Godshill itself, in Rookley there arose a Methodist Chapel, at Roud a Baptist
Chapel and at Sandford a Bible Christian (now Methodist) Chapel. In 1863, Mr
John Woodward established a school at Rookley to which on his death he added
further endowment.

It is hard to escape the conclusion that the status of the Vicar of Godshill had
diminished through two changes: the growth of Non-conformity and the growth of
powers vested in secular local government

FIFTEEN
THE SEWELL FAMILY

In or soon after 1755, the non-resident Vicar of Godshill the Revd William appointed to exercise care of Godshill parish as his Curate the Revd W Sewell, a man descended from a family of Westmorland gentry. It was not a of religious fervour in the Church of England, and Mr Sewell seems to have be eccentric almost to the point of oddity. He did however obtain the consent of well-known Newport Solicitor (Robert Clarke) to the hand in marriage of hi daughter aged 19, much younger than himself. As Robert Clarke was well-established in his profession, there must have been some surprise at the difference in social status, and this was held to be a good match for a 'mere' curate. The Rev William Sewell resigned in 1763 and he and his young wife left the Island to take up his incumbency on the borders of Hampshire and Berkshire. From this unremarkable beginning sprang substantial results.

In 1775 a son Thomas was born to William Sewell and his wife. In due course Thomas returned to the Island to be articled to his maternal uncle Richard Clarke who had become Senior Partner in the family legal firm in Newport in succession to Robert. Incidentally, Richard Clarke was much involved in the publication in 1781 of the History of the Island with Sir Richard Worsley. In due course Thomas qualified as a Solicitor, married his cousin Jane the daughter of a local clergyman, and himself became a partner in the firm. Thomas Sewell rose to influential posts on the Island: he was Solicitor and Political Agent to the Earl of Yarborough, who had married the heiress of the Appuldurcombe Estate. He also became Recorder of Newport, and later (in 1838/40) Mayor of the town.

In 1820 the firm, then 'Sewell, Hearn and Sewell' moved to a handsome red - brick building in Newport High Street. However his opposition to the Reform Bill laid Thomas Sewell open to militant and indeed riotous attack and the windows of his house were smashed by the mob. Though seventy-four years had elapsed since his father had served there as curate, Thomas Sewell had maintained links with Godshill. For example, the Minutes of a meeting of Godshill Vestry show that he was acting for that body in 1837. (The business related to the appointment of a Valuer in connection with rating and Tithe commutation under two of the statutes passed in this reforming period.)

His life ended unhappily, both materially following his extravagance and perhaps the failure of two local banks, and in health for he was afflicted by gout. He died in 1842. It was said that it took the family and the firm thirty years to clear his debts. His daughter Elizabeth later drew attention to the generous hospitality that was the norm in their home, with a great deal of coming and going by persons of all ranks, from Lord Yarborough to men of business and farmers. There would not have been the separation of legal practice from personal and family life that is normal today, and moreover anyone in public life was expected to entertain his supporters. Elizabeth recorded on a more personal note that, although he was kind to his children, he was 'outwardly cold' and capable of being 'irritable in manner'.

' his wife had 12 children, of whom nine reached maturity. Five
¬ of the former curate of Godshill, were in due course
.eature in the Dictionary of National Biography.

,oorn 1815) was a dedicated Anglican, influenced by the Oxford
,er of religious works and a teacher. She took private pupils for
.rs, and in 1866 founded St Boniface School in Ventnor for Middle-

(born 1810) graduated from New College Oxford, became a Fellow and
.en of that College, Doctor of Divinity and ultimately Vice-Chancellor of the
.iversity.

William (born 1804) also went up to Oxford, was ordained, became prominent in
the Oxford Movement and founded both Radley School in Berkshire and St
Columbus College Dublin.

Richard (born 1803) went from Winchester School to Magdalene Oxford to study
law, and while there won the Newdigate Prize for composing poetry. After being
called to the Bar, he emigrated to Australia and was an academic lawyer at
Melbourne University.

Henry was a Solicitor and his life is outlined below.

(Robert (born 1807) also became a Solicitor, but died young.)

From 1825 to 1837, as was discovered after his death, Thomas Sewell kept a
private account book, which revealed much about his life in his fifties and early
sixties

Extracts from the accounts are revealing.
1827 180 dozen bottles of wine purchased of which
     38 dozen were consumed during the year.
     12 butts of sherry (each 130 gallons) plus
     74 pipes of port (each 105 gallons)

1828 New wine cellars were taken into use.
     558 bottles of wine were consumed
1829 822 bottles were consumed
1830 824 bottles were consumed
1831 408 bottles were consumed-

After this there are no such records.

(From this point [1990] inflation is assumed of a factor of 50, but the multiplied
figures given are necessarily approximate and must be treated with caution. The
actual figures are not set out.)

Thomas Sewell was also a lover of horses. For his horses, their food equipment
and other items, (modern values) about £1,500.

Purchase of a horse, (modern values) about a modest £100.
Purchase of 2 horses, one from Wales, (modern values) together about £2
Disbursements during the year on horses, (modern values) about £8,000.

Substantial sums were disbursed by Thomas Sewell for the education
qualification of his sons and of Elizabeth, though not for other daughters. Aga
modem values: admission to the Bar for Richard cost approximately £6,500
payment to the same son in 1833 would today be worth £20,000, and s
Robert's Articles of Clerkship (cf apprenticeship) in 1828 cost the equal today
£6,000.

Thomas Sewell's Account Book records disbursements for dental treatment for his
wife, and for her and the daughters: dancing lessons, bonnets, clogs, umbrellas,
gowns, scent, gloves, shoes, shawls, turban handkerchiefs and ribbons.

He spent heavily on books, though it is unclear whether this was a law library for
the practice, domestic and educational for the children or a collection of
expensively bound volumes for his private study. The main expenditure was in
1827, the first year of the Account Book, but with smaller amounts in 1828 and
1829 in three years in modern values he spent about £33,000.

Household expenses include Well Diggers and 'gass' lights, an indication that
Newport was following the latest arrangements for domestic comfort. Candlesticks
were still needed, no doubt in bedrooms and an expensive one was purchased.
The privy too had to be emptied at not inconsiderable cost.

One important indication of ease and status was the keeping of a coach, and the
accounts include an item for repair.

It was perhaps for the easing of his gout that Thomas Sewell bought air pillows.

Music played an important part in the professional classes' domestic life, and the
home contained both a piano and an organ.

The household was run by five servants, and the cost of their wages in 1827 was
about 11% of the household budget, with the highest paid receiving four times the
lowest. They were paid quarterly, four females and one male who eventually rose
to butler.

Mr Sewell was certainly not extravagant during these years in respect of his own
dress, although he did like a new hat each year. He wore knee-breeches with
stockings and buckled shoes with gaiters in cold or wet weather. He wore
spectacles, and quite a major item was his razors.

It would not be surprising to find in a professional man of those days a significant
outlay on gambling. There is however only a single entry in these years: 'cards'. It
is possible that he kept a tally elsewhere and only entered a yearly total when out
of pocket in aggregate, and that all the other years he was in pocket.

Godshill would have been made on horseback in reasonable ~s for longer journeys he would hire a one horse light two- . fly. Some travellers on that road would hire a boy to open ∠tes that were encountered on the way.

∠ies Thomas Sewell supported were the Society for Promoting √ledge (SPCK), the Bible Society, the Newport Charity Sermon, and ∠ay Schools in and around Newport (which may well have included All these were Anglican. The family also contributed to the Hospital, ∠ools and the Mechanics Institute, and his Accounts show donations to the ∠ng lectures, the Coal Committee, the Agricultural Society, the Geological ∠ciety, the Choral Society, the Cricket Club and the Archery Club. On one ∠ccasion he paid for fishing at Sandown.

He recorded in 1837 that 'an election dinner cost him' (in modern values about) £600.

There were of course Poor Rates and Church Rates. When his son Thomas died aged 20, the funeral for 'my dearest Tom' was clearly a splendid affair, with cost to match.

It is no surprise to find his total annual expenditure (using the same artificial multiplier as before) as fluctuating in the years 1827 to 1837 in the range in modern values of £140,000/£200,000.

Henry Sewell

When Thomas Sewell, son of the Godshill Curate, died in 1842, his fourth son Henry had long since passed through his time as an articled clerk in the family firm and qualified. In 1834 he had married Lucinda Nedham, and in due course they had six children. He was a busy market town Solicitor, living first in Lugley Cottage Newport and later in a gloomy Manor House named Pidford, near Rookley and just outside the boundary of Godshill Parish. On the death of his father, he was appointed to two of his father's public offices for the Isle of Wight: Deputy Governor and Her Majesty's Coroner. Lucinda was not in good health, and for that reason the household, which included Henry's widowed Mother and his four unmarried sisters with Henry's five children, all moved to Ventnor in 1844.

After giving birth to her 6th child, Lucinda died. Henry resigned from his firm and his public offices and left the Island. He was never to return. It was later learnt that that he had very little contact with his family thereafter.

Henry moved to London, and by the late 1840s he was involved in the affairs of an Anglican foundation promoting emigration to New Zealand. He went out to South Island N.Z. on behalf of this foundation arriving early in 1853, and liking the country, stayed on when his task was concluded, continuing to practice as a Solicitor. He was elected both to the Provincial Council and as Member for Christchurch in the House of Representatives. It was a time of political upheaval in the colony, the Maori population being disenchanted with their new position, and white New Zealanders being disenchanted with Westminster. In 1854, Henry

Sewell became Solicitor General on a small Council, but this oligarchy lasted only two months, before being brought down by the resignation of Sewell, who with his two colleagues on the House of Representatives, was seeking more democratic government. The Governor who succeeded, invited Henry Sewell to form and lead the new Government in this first democratically elected Parliament. His programme for administering the colony was twice defeated by a small majority, and he was out of office in 1856 after a very short tenure.

He married again, but in 1876 he and his wife decided to move to England. He died three years later, and was buried at Waresley, a village west of Cambridge. A gift in his memory is recorded in Ventnor (IoW) Church by three of his unmarried sisters, who had been left to bring up his children there. Henry Sewell was clearly an able man and a man of culture whose conversation 'sparkled with cleverness and wit'. However, he was also volatile, 'fussy' and restless, and he was criticised as being 'too easily impressionable, and full of false alarms'. So ended the life of a grandson of that curate who had served for several years in Godshill.

O
LIGHTNING STRIKES

Realisation of the need for a lightning conductor on a prominent church tower is, one supposes, relatively recent. Certainly the tower of Godshill Church was struck on three separate occasions in the space of 126 years.

About 9 o'clock one Monday morning in January 1778, the church tower was struck about four feet below the clock-dial. The force of the discharge tore off large pieces of stone and loosened many others. It broke the clock-face, melted the upper part of the pendulum, distorted the works of the clock and broke the piece of iron that regulated the striking. The force of the strike split the tower wall on the south side and loosened battlements. The spindle that supported the weathercock was bent double, and some of the roofing lead was rolled up. Pinnacles were affected, with their cramp-irons and lead wrenched out. The glass in the great window behind the gallery was shattered and its frame loosened and partly torn off. There was a large hole at the valley between the two roofs at the west end. Inside the church, there was some damage, and several routes to earth could be traced, one the full length of the church right to the east end, terminating in furrows in the ground outside.

All this we know from a detailed note written by the Curate Daniel Walsh in Godshill on 21st January 1778 to inform Sir Richard Worsley a short while after the happening.

Much of the repair work would have been done by local craftsmen, but a bill has survived in relation to the mostly specialised work for a new weather-vane.

Pd for new vane for the Tower	£9 . 8s . 0d
Cartage of do. From London	6 . 4d
For bringing the Pole for the Vane	1 . 0d
Paid for paintg the Vane Pole	4 . 7d

There was a further strike in 1897, five years into the incumbency of the Revd Pemberton Bartlett, which caused damage both outside and inside the structure. A first inspection showed that a pinnacle on the western end was dislodged, and it was clear that major repairs would be needed. Plans were put in hand.

In the summer of 1904, a third lightning strike was suffered. The upper storey of the Tower, built early in the 17th century, was destroyed, the clock being found on the path below. There was serious internal damage. Renovation work was already in hand. In a strange way this third strike seems to have accelerated the repair work and by the end of the year work on the fabric had been completed.

SIXTEEN
GODSHILL ABOUT 1867

We might imagine the Revd T Ratcliffe taking a walk around the village to the care of which he had just been inducted in 1867.
At the top of the hill near the Church
    The Bell Inn with Dairy attached
    4 thatched cottages (this group of buildings had at that time a poor reputation. The inhabitants were described as untidy, disorderly and slovenly). The Bell and these cottages are reliably dated back to the 16th century.
    Pound Cottage with the Pound behind for enclosing stray animals
    Standen Cottage

From Church Hill down to The Square ran Church Shute Hollow, a Chine rough and unmetalled, with overhanging tree-branches. There was often a swift-flowing stream, and indeed there is still a spring at the top of the hill.

Another way down was to the School, by a grassy tree-sheltered path known as School Chine, to the north of the Church. (An alternative when visiting outlying parts of the parish would be to walk or ride southwards along Sainham Lane, then Love Lane, past Sheepwash Farm and Stenbury Manor, finally coming to the village of Whitwell.)

Next was Stone Cross Cottage which had been the home of several of the Curates prior to Thomas Ratcliffe becoming resident incumbent. The next cottage was 'The Hollies'. The neighbouring property to the north was the Blacksmith's Forge and his cottage. Further north was a complex including a thatched cottage comprising Louisa Leal's Bakehouse and Cottage. She was a popular personality with a flourishing business. The next properties were two thatched cottages, one housing a family of labourers and beyond that a cottage fronting onto the Square occupied by Daniel Morris. Further on were two Cottages, one named Wisteria, and then an odd-shaped dwelling named after a family who had earlier had it: the Wrong family.

Beyond Wrongs Cottage was an unbuilt area over which one could reach what local people called 'the Bog'. One next came to a small thatched cottage and then the School, commissioned by Lord Yarborough, and the separate School House.

***

All over the country the big estates were being broken up and farms sold. In the parish of Godshill, Gatcombe Farm, Park Farm, Sheepwash Farm, Stenbury Manor Farm, Lessland Farm, Moor Farm, Bridgecourt and Bridge Farms: all became legal entities separate from Appuldurcombe. The consequence was socially confusing and a fluid labour market resulted.

Bridge Farm was owned at the turn of the century by three men, one living in Guildford, one in Essex and the third in the Temple (London). The tenant was John Frederick Attrill who also owned Upper Appleford Farm. There were several labourers' cottages at Bridge Farm, and two of the men were named Walter Hollis and Leonard Charles Sievier.

Bridge Court Farm was farmed by Frederick Kemp and among his labourers nearby were Frederick Eglington and Harry Orchard. The Watermill was owned and worked by George Henry Burt who lived at the Mill Cottage.

Nearby was Lavenders, a small farm farmed by William Austin.

Bagwich Farm was in the hands of one of the Morris family.
Beacon Alley ran up the hill then, as now, between steep banks and overhanging trees. Hidden away were two cottages, one occupied by Henry Butt, the other by Reginald Surrey-Lane or Surrey-Love.

Bleakdown Farm was occupied and worked by Frederick George Butchers, with cottages lived in by Fred Rolf and Charles Henry Toms.

In Roud Hamlet was Holden farm occupied by one of the Hollis family, and another Hollis farmed Orchard Farm.

There were scattered cottages at Merryl, named after a landowner who lived in Whitwell, and at Millbank and Itchall near Stenbury Manor.

Also outside the centre of the village were :

Stone Cottage	a farm labourer
Dubbers	a house with a large piece of land
Scotland Farm	owned by the Hayles family who lived at Appleford
Lower Elliots Farm	occupied by the Langdon Family

The Manors

In the 19th century, Appleford Manor passed into the hands of a non-resident family, the Bonham-Carters, and thus a long connection of its owners with All Saints came to an end. In the 18th century the owner had been William Pike, prominent on the Vestry.

Bridge Court Manor was Crown property for several centuries and the home of the Meux family until the death in 1638 of Sir William Meux. There was a history of efficient farming and milling, and the remains of the Watermill may still be seen. Then the Coleman family were there. By the late 19th Century it was owned by Mr Frank Barton. Marshy ground nearby was famous for withies for thatching, and rushes for lights.

Bagwich (Abaginge) It was recorded as a lod or small estate before the Norman Conquest. It came into the estates of the de Redvers and in the 12th century was granted to Christchurch Priory Twyneham. Bagwich is thought to mean 'Dairy Farm round the back of the Church'. By the Dissolution it appears to have been absorbed into the Manor of Apse (near Newchurch IoW) owned by the same Priory. In 1603 the two were in common lay ownership in the Rice family. From them Bagwich passed to Thomas Macham and then to the Miller family who were well known on the Island. Sir Thomas Miller Bt was owner until 1723 when the estate was conveyed to Joachim Peterson. However by 1780 rent is recorded as being paid to the Crown. The surnames of both the Bull family and of Thomas Whitewood (owner in 1827) are mentioned above (Section 11). The property at some point became glebeland for the parish of Wootton.

Kennerly Manor, which had in the past produced benefactors such as Peter Garde and John Casford, had by the late 19th century been dismantled. Most of the Manor buildings had been demolished and the land disposed of piecemeal. A house called Little Kennerly was later owned by Mr F A Joyce.

Lessland was another anciently prominent manor which had come to little by the 1860s. The owner then, Mr J C Tompkins also owned Rew Manor Farm within Godshill parish.

Roud Manor was a free manor in the time of Edward the Confessor, mid 11th century, and later passed into the hands of the de Lisle family based in Wootton and ultimately to the,Worsleys of Appuldurcombe, who sold it off to Mr Arthur Atherly.

Sandford Manor was given to the Norman Abbey of Montesbourg by mid 12th century, as is recorded in a Papal record. The deeds have been lost but it was integrated into the Appuldurcombe Estate early in the 19th century.   Lord Yarborough sold Sandford Manor to Mr Michael Spartali in 1872.

Rookley Manor was granted to the Norman family de Insula. Men and women with the surname Rookley appear on documents for many years, and in 1346 Geoffrey Rookley agreed to pay to the Crown a substantial annual sum for the right to establish an Oratory Chapel at the Manor. The Coke/Cooke family with others were involved from 1428 to 1519, after which the ownership passed to the Bannister and Meux families of Kingston for well over a century. The Colemans of Bridge Court were farming part of the estate before it was bought by the Worsleys of Appuldurcombe. Again it was sold off and in 1863 Mr John Woodward established a school at Rookley.

Bleakdown (also known as Blakesdon) was around 1300 transferred from the de Lisle family to Christchurch Priory. It may have been one of those properties that the Crown retained, since some kind of grant was made in 1624/25 to Mr Edward Ramsey and others, but in 1780 it was to the Crown that Mr William Thatcher paid rent. Bleakdown was owned in 1900 by Mr Arthur Atherley, still within Godshill parish.

What is today known as Munsley Farm, has carried various variations of name, sometimes including the word 'Hill'. It stands on the edge of a marshy peat area known locally as 'the Bog'. From around 1300 it has formed part of Bridge Court Manor.

Week. in the south of the parish was one of the properties that passed from lay Norman hands to the Benedictine house of Montesbourg. Later it formed part of Appyldurcombe Estate, but in 1855 Lord Yarborough retained it for the Anderson-Pelhams. For many years its windmill was a source of income. At Whiteley Bank a water-mill was equally long-established, and indeed the estate is known as French Mill.

P
SOME GODSHILL RESIDENTS about 1900

Abbot, James: the father of 14 healthy children, worked at Park Farm.
Atkey, James Henry: lived at Church Hill Cottage. Village Blacksmith.
Attrill, Frank: thatched Cottage at Scotland Corner.
    Dealt in poultry, and drove ponytrap.
Attrill, Nathaniel: Church Hill Cottages, where he and wife Elizabeth
    kept a few cows and sold milk, & also cigarettes.
    Daughter 'Addy' became School-teacher.
Austin, William: farmed Lavenders Farm, related to William Cheverton.
Bartlett, Alicia: Stone Cross Cottage, High Street with her husband the Vicar.
Bellman, William: worked at Sheepwash Farm. Lost a leg in shooting accident.
Blunt, James: Proprietor with wife of Essex Cottage Teashop before Mrs Kemp.
Buckle, Matthew: Landlord of the Griffin,
    a Scot who married an Island girl nee Haydon.

Burt, George Henry: Miller at Bridgecourt. Children loved to watch him at work.

Cheverton, Austin: Lavenders

Cheverton, William: farmed Upper Elliotts Farm. Arthur = nephew

Clarkson, Francis William: Baker at property now Doll Museum (Welcomes).

Coward, Robert: Seafarer. Smithy Cottage (part) & Bakehouse in Square.

Crook, John: Wisteria, Postmaster & owner of General Stores.

Daniel, Laverna: Village Schoolmistress

Denham, Henry Walter: Farmed Godshill Park Farm

Dennis, George Henry: Pound Cottage. Kept cows, ran dairy with wife Jenny.
    Daughter = Elsie.

Eglington, Frederick of Bridgecourt Farm Cottage. His wife was Verger at All
Saints for many years. On his death she moved to Webster's Cottage opposite the
School, and lived to very old age.

Eldridge, Cornelius: Farmworker living at Dubbers Well House

Goodchild, Thomas: Farmed Scotland Farm. Jack = Grandson

Griffin, James Henry: Cottage in High Street, Shoe Mender and Postman.

Griffin, Mercy: Mother-in-law of G H Dennis. Pound Cottage too.

Hayles, Ernest Ingram: Dubbers. Housebuilder, emigrated to Australia. Methodist.

Hollis, Sidney Mearman: Farm Cottage in High Street.
    Ran a dairy and delivered milk from churn fitted to bicycle.

Hollis, Walter: Bridge Farm Cottage, & later West Street where he kept
    a few cows and ran a small dairy. Children were interested to see him
    draw water from well inside his cottage.

Humby, Henry James: Landlord of 'Bell' Inn.

Kemp, Frederick: farmed Bridgecourt Farm. His wife ran 'Essex Cottage' teashop.

Langdon, Edward Herbert: owned major part of Lower Elliotts Farm,
    which he farmed. Loyal Churchman, gave shows with his Magic Lantern.

Leal, Louisa: ran tea-garden at Bakehouse in High Street.
    Daughter Ida married William Morris, later sub-Postmaster.

Mew, Charles Henry: Farmworker at Sheepwash Farm

Morris, Daniel: Carpenter Builder & Undertaker. Methodist.

Morris, Frederick: Farmer, first at Sheepwash Farm, later Bagwich Farm.

Morris, Henry: Syringa in the Square and the Bats-wing shop.
    His son married 'Tops' Morris who lived at Syringa.

Ratcliffe: Former Vicar's family lived at his house (now 'Model Village').

Roylance, Agnes: Wrongs Cottage. A widow who lived with her daughter

Russell, Frederick: Village Policeman living next to Village Hall.

Sievier, Leonard Charles: Farmworker at Bridge Farm where he lived in cottage.

Simpkins, Sarah: Church Gate Cottage, related to Dennis family.

Stevens, Ada (widow) & Maud: The Hollies. Maud, Church Organist
    for 60 years, including RC Church Ventnor.
    Cellist & organiser of Concerts.

Tutton, Edward (Teddy): farm-worker at Scotland Corner

Winter, Charles: Forge Cottage High Street, Market Gardener
    (Smithy Car Park now).

SEVENTEEN
ALL SAINTS CHURCH and GODSHILL LIFE to 1904

In Thomas Ratcliffe's time Godshill Church was already known to many as the Church of the Lily Cross. In 1842, this unique and beautiful secco painting on the wall of the south transept was discovered by the Curate the Rev W L Girandot by accident, for it had earlier been totally covered. It was probably the work of at least one Italian painter of the early 16th century. This date coincided with the conversion of this part of the church to a Chantry Chapel by Sir John Leigh. Once restored, it needed protection from sunlight.

Thomas Ratcliffe was incumbent from 1867 for 25 years. He enjoyed wealth from investment in South American Railways. He bought from Queens College Oxford the glebe including the very house which the Rev Henry Worsley had controversially created in 1821 (see Section 13.) There he lived with his family.

At the time of his arrival, the interior of All Saints Church Godshill was quite different from today, and not in good condition. The 'false' lathe-&-plaster ceiling installed in 1751 obscured the 15th century roof timbers, and whitewash covered many walls. In the south transept stood the immense stone sarcophagus of 1822 ('the Tub'). Where the High Altar now stands within its sanctuary on the south side had since 1846 stood the huge family pew of the Worsleys of Appuldurcombe. The pipe-organ installed in 1814 was by 1867 in neglected condition, reflected in a 'wheezy' tone.

Church plate
In the Parish Chest at Thomas Ratcliffe's arrival in 1867, along with the Registers and other documents was the Church silverware:

Two chalices with matching patens dated 1641/42 are inscribed round the base of each chalice: 'Provided by Ri Legg Tho Norrice Churchwardens - - - Crosfield Vicar and the rest of ye parishioners of Goddeshull Anno Domino 1642'. Each paten is inscribed:'T E+CVP+Of+ Gods + Hil Parish' (The First Civil War began in 1642.)

A silver Flagon with cover is inscribed: 'Gift of Sir Robert Worsley Bart to the church of Godshill April 1705'.

Another silver Flagon with cover is from 1739/40 and is inscribed: 'The gift of Charles Worsley Esq to the parish of Godshill in the Isle of Wight IHS' + the Worsley Arms.

A silver Chalice and Paten also presented by Charles Worsley, both inscribed 1739/40.

In 1874, Mr Ratcliffe received from Colonel Maiden a silver Cup.

Paintings
One of the attractions to All Saints Godshill was the painting 'Daniel in the Lions' Den'. This had been donated to the church by Lord Yarborough when he was

dispersing the Worsley collection in mid-century (see section 12). It had always been attributed to Rubens (1577 -1640), but difference of opinion among experts brought it to the public attention and increased the number of visitors to the church. From 1880 it was generally conceded to be a copy made within Rubens' School. Above the north door, and thus immediately in view to all those who entered from the south door, was a medieval fresco of 'The Day of Judgment', but by 1846 it was in faded and dilapidated condition, and the new acquisition was hung over it.

The Duke de Moro was one of the five-man Committee which organised the Restoration. In 1897 he presented a painting: <u>Madonna and Child dated 1630 by Tiorelli</u>. (One previous owner was the infamous Count Alfred Guillaume Gabriel d'Orsay (1801 - 52) who died in a drunken brawl and whose wife later married the Earl of Blessington, becoming famous for her literary salon in London.)

There were other gifts: in 1881, Lord Yarborough donated the cost of renovating the South Porch, and there were gifts of smaller items at this time of refurbishment of the church. Later, a window in the south chancel was filled with stained glass, as a memorial to the Vicar the Revd Thomas Ratcliffe.

This was a time of some prosperity on the Island from what today might be called 'tourism'. Several factors made the Island more attractive to visitors. The presence of the Queen at Osborne House had an effect. Easier transport helped: both the improved state of the roads and the new railway system, first on the mainland, and then supplemented in 1862 by the opening of the line from Cowes to Newport. The railway came in due course also to Shanklin. Another quite short journey by road took the visitor to and from Godshill.

Meanwhile democracy took a further step in 1888 with widened voting franchise for local governing bodies, and correspondingly reduced power for the Church Vestry.

***

When the Revd Thomas Ratcliffe died in 1892, the Revd Pemberton R H Bartlett was presented by Queens College Oxford and duly inducted as Vicar. As his predecessor owned the house in which he had lived, the new Vicar had to be accommodated elsewhere, and moved into Stone Cross Cottage, between the Methodist Chapel and the Forge. Mr Ratcliffe had been highly respected as an authoritarian leader for 25 years, and his family still lived in Godshill High Street, but the new Vicar was able to establish himself. Among the friendships he formed was one with Capt H M Worsley by then retired. The Worsley family may have gone from Appuldurcombe, but this member of another branch maintained his interest in All Saints Church. Mr Bartlett continued as Vicar until 1932.

At the outset of his ministry, he recorded of the Church building that it had 'happily escaped restoration in the modern sense'. Plans were laid and a Restoration Fund was started. The two friends produced a written short Guide to the Church in 1898. They wrote that it was 'needless to call attention to the dilapidated condition' of the church. Its walls were 'so uneven that no amount of sweeping (could) keep them clean. The windows badly wanted repairing. The plaster ceiling which (had) covered the ancient roof beams since the year 1751 (required) to be removed'. The box-pews were in dire need of replacing: neither conducive to worship nor having historical interest, being as recent as 1846. The repairs felt to be needed was 'conservative renovation'. Work should be put in hand as soon as funds were raised 'unless the Church is to become an absolute ruin' wrote the Rev Mr Bartlett and Captain Worsley. All profits from the sale of the Guide (6d) were to be devoted to the Restoration Fund. Then in 1897 the tower was struck by lightning.

In the Summer of 1904, the Tower suffered its third lightning strike. The repair work proceeded apace with a replacement top level to the tower and a missing pinnacle replaced. The damaged clock was restored. The planned changes inside the Church were implemented, including the removal of the 1750s ceiling, and the removal of the galleries. The wall-paintings were restored. The Worsley sarcophagus was moved from the South Transept to its present position. Incidentally, when it was dismantled for the purpose, the names of the workmen who first erected it were found pencilled on one of the inner pieces, but no copy was taken of those names.

Features in that transept became visible, and visitors still enjoy the carved stone heads of the corbels, and the wooden figures. Might some perhaps represent the nuns of the London house which once had rights over Appuldurcombe?

The massive 15th century South door was painstakingly cleaned of obsolete notices, old paint, grime and rust. Incidentally, the lock was still in working order, and thus the 12-inch-long medieval iron key was still in use, weighing 1lb 7oz. A new lock was however added, with a shorter (but heavier) key. Of the two hinges, the top one is original, although the lower one is a later copy. Also original are the twisted sanctuary ring and plate which are seen behind the door.

The work on the fabric was completed in 1904.

The recommended access to the Church was up the steps from the direction of the Square past the remains of the Churchyard Cross (in 1797 turned into a sundial), rather than by way of the thatched cottages on the Hill and past the spot where the parish stocks had stood. This suggests that the writers were avoiding visitors being affronted by the unkempt condition of those cottages (so trim and photogenic today). At the bottom of the steps 'bicycles will be safe and carriages can wait with greater convenience than on the Hill.'

***

Population numbers are known from the 10-year Census started in 1801. Numbers in Godshill rose substantially each decade from 1801 (1,079) to 1841 (1,435). They then fell each decade to 1871 (1,197) and rose to their highest in 1891 (1,480) before falling again. The increase in population numbers on the whole Island rose even more sharply between 1811 and 1881; in the former year Godshill had 4.7% of the Island population, but 70 years later this had dropped to 1.8%.

One of the continuing changes of this time was the increase in secular local government and the corresponding diminution of the power and responsibility of the Incumbent and the Vestry. The Isle of Wight had a County Council and Godshill had a secular Parish Council. This shift was neatly demonstrated in a confrontation. For centuries, the Vicar and Churchwardens had been responsible for the safe custody, in the Parish Chest within the Church, of legal documents such as Registers and (since about 1840) the parish's copy of the Tithe Map and Apportionments. (The latter is the text giving factual data). Now that the Parish had its new Council, who should hold the Tithe documents? There was added point in respect of the Tithe documents because the payment aroused strong feelings in payers, and was for the Vicar an important part of his income. Bitter correspondence failed to produce agreement, and the issue was referred some time after 1894 for adjudication by the County Council at a Special Meeting held at the Guildhall Newport. The decision, following a similar case on the mainland, was that the right to direct where these documents should be deposited should belong to the Parish Council, and not to the Church.

Another major change was the coming of the Railway to the village of Godshill in 1897, the line running from Merstone Junction to St Lawrence. The route of the railway may be traced on the ground, where embankments, cuttings and the bases of bridges are still visible, and on a large-scale modern map. The line came almost due south, passing to the west of Munsley Farm, swinging around the village by Scotland Farm and then due south almost to Whitwell, before passing to the east of that village and to St Lawrence. A separate line from Shanklin served Ventnor. This new mode of travel had clear advantages over horse-drawn conveyance and bicycle, and accelerated the rate of social change for Godshill.

One visitor wrote of how on alighting at the little Railway Station at Godshill, he found a path that led across one or two pleasant green fields, straight to All Saints Church. He visited the Essex Cottage to take tea, and was informed by the Morrises that Princess Beatrice, daughter of Queen Victoria, who then lived at Osborne House, had taken tea there. A writer, Alan Tarbat, described Godshill as 'The Queen of Villages', but regretted the destruction of the old 'Poor House' and of other ancient buildings when he walked down from Scotland Corner.

In 1887, a new peal of bells had replaced the six bells which had been cast in 1822 after the previous four had been melted down. On 31st December 1899, the Godshill Ringers pealed out the 1800s and pealed in the 1900s, which they did again on the 31st December 1999.

***

The 1890s had not been an easy time for the Island. After a drive from Osborne House (IoW) the elderly Queen Victoria wrote in her diary following a disastrous harvest: 'Not a blade of grass, the potatoes destroyed, the turnips gone wrong, the oats fit for nothing, no food for the cattle, and no means of selling them'.

SOME MORE GODSHILL RESIDENTS
Additional names & addresses from Register of Electors 1st January 1915

Attrill	Frank	Mews Farm, Sandford
Attrill	Frederick J	Upper Appleford farm
Barton	Elizabeth	South View
Bellman	John	Sheepwash Farm
Booker	Thomas	Sandford
Booker	George	Holden Cottage, Roud
Butchers	Frederick G	Bleakdown Farm
Butchers	Frederick J	Itchell, near Stenbury
Butt	Henry	Beacon Alley
Cake	Frederick W	Lessland Farm Cotts
Calloway	Charlotte	West Street
Calloway	John	?
Calloway	Ernest	Moor Farm
Cheek	Harry	Millbank House
Chiverton	Charlie	1, Millbank Cottages
Chiverton	Charlie	Bobberstone
Crutcher	James	Merryl
Daniel	Laverna	School House
Deadman	Frederick W	Railway Station
Dennis	Alfred	?
Dennis	Harry	Lower Bohemia
Draper	Isaac	Froghill
Dyer	James	Appleford Farm Cott
Dyer	James W	Sandford
Edmunds	Charles	Sheepwash Farm
Edmunds	Edward J	Great Kennerley
Fiander	William	Lodwell Farm ?????
Gladdis	George	Upper Appleford Cotts
Guy	Harry	Rosedene, Sandford o/o
Guy	Maurice	?
Harrlson	Ricardo	The Stone Cottage
Hayden	Edward	?
Hayles	Oliver A	Appleford Farm o/o
Hayles	Oliver	Pagham & Scotland Farms
Hills	Henry	Cypress Cott
Hills	William	Sandford
Hollis	Thomas	Orchards Farm
Hollis	Herbert	Holden farm
Hollis	Samuel	Calloways farm
Jones	William J	?
Kingswell	Gaius	?
Lacey	James E	Upper Appleford Cott
Lane	Reginald S	The Beacon

Larcombe	John	Appleford Farm Cotts
Leal	Frank	(lodger) High Street
Legg	John	Myrtle Cottage, Rookley
Mew	William H	Sandford Farm
Miles	Frederick J	Sheepwash Dairy
Morris	Edwin	Bagwich Farm
Morris	Henry J	Appledurcombe Dairy
Morris	Frank W	West Street
Morris	Thomas H	Redhill farm
Orchard	Charles H	Bathingbourne Farm Cotts
Orchard	Harry	Bridgecourt Farm Cotts
Orchard	Frank	Wrongs Cottage
Parsons	Bernard G	Kennerley farm
Payne	Clement	Bohemia Comer
Peach	Jane A M	West Street
Phillips	Eli	?
Plumbley	William	Scotland Corner
Read	Frederick	Cottage, Sandford
Reynolds	George	?
Reynolds	Minnie	Park Wall
Ringer	Francis A	Sunnyside
Rolf	Frederick J	Upper Yard
Rolf	Fred	Bleakdown
Rolf	George	Lower Yard Farm
Rolf	Walter H	Kennerley Farm
Rowson	John	West Street
Rowson	Frederick R	Montrose
Ryall	George	Great Kennerley
Scot	Percival H	Gatcliff farm
Scovell	Alfred	Lower Bohemia
Scovell	James	New Barn, Stenbury
Sibbick	James	Sandford
Sibbick	William H	Sandford
Sleep	Charles	Shamrock Cottage
Sleep	Henry C	South View
Squibb	George	Sandford
Squibb	Jeremiah	Millbank Cottages, Sandford
Taylor	Charles H	West View
Thorne	Edward	?
Thorne	Thomas	The Hut, Appleford
Thorne	William	North Appleford
Toms	Charles H	Bleak Down
Turner	Albert	Appleford Farm cott
Urry.	George W	Freemantles
Warder	Ivan E	French Mills, Sandford
Way	Charles	Bank Cottage
Westmore	George	North Appleford

White	James	?
Whittington	William	Mumfords
Wicket	Herbert J	Rookley farm
Young	George	Summersbury
Young	James	Sandford

APPENDIX 1
ALL SAINTS. GODSHILL
a summary for a visit

Never ask how old a church is! The great majority of English Churches are not of a single period in their fabric, but show a series of re-buildings, extensions and amendments in the style then current, and moreover with furnishings, goods and ornaments of a succession of periods. Indeed, many are built on the sites of earlier buildings which have few traces visible, or none. Here at Godshill a detached fragment of a Norman capital survives, and some stone has been re-used with dog-tooth moulding. Otherwise the oldest visible item is the font (13th century with its much later Jacobean cover). The processional cross is C14th, from Italy.

After the Norman building of the first stone church, All Saints was almost entirely rebuilt twice, and thus in two styles. Some of the earlier re-build in Decorated work remains (1300 to 1375) such as the tracery in the two east windows, and the transept arches, but otherwise most of what is visible is from the later re-build in Perpendicular style (1375 to 1485). This latter is considered particularly fine.

To gain a sense of the shape of the Church, the ideal view would be from the air, but one has to be content with a walk around the outside. Ignoring the tower, the church comprises two ranges of equal length, long in relation to width and with long unbroken roofs. There is (unusually) no outward distinction of chancel from nave. The east end with double gable shows the two components most clearly. Halfway down each side is a transept or cross-arm, neatly gabled in. The western half of the south side is then halved again by the porch. The tower is the width of the north range, and extends it.

One cannot judge a Church by lists of noteworthy artefacts, but the visitor should also be aware of:
a fine Jacobean altar table (1631) in the north transept;
the painted Commandment Boards (1662),
the 1529 Leigh monument between the Chancel and the north chapel;
two mural paintings: the C15th 'Christ of the lilies' in the south transept,
                        and the medieval consecration cross with pointing hand
                            on the south chancel wall.

two oil paintings: in the south transept a Tiorelli 'Virgin & Child',
and on the north wall 'Daniel in the Lions' Den'
of the School of Rubens

Outside, the Tower is widely admired. The upper stages have been rebuilt following lightning damage (see section 0).

There are, of course, many other things of interest, as a full Guide will reveal. As for the situation of the church, its knoll elevates it in view from considerable distances.

What one can see in stone is only part of the story, for the true history is what has gone on within the building and the surrounding churchyard. Moreover, there is every reason to suppose that Christian worship on this spot has been continuous for well over 1000 years, and for centuries before everything in stone that is visible today.

APPENDIX 2
SUMMARY OF SOME TRANSACTIONS

'The Cartulary of Carisbrooke Priory' by Dom G F Hockey

c. 1140   Baldwin Earl of Devon & Lord of the Isle of Wight confirmed to the
Abbot
          of Lyra the appropriation of Godshill Church as arranged by William
Fitz
          Osbern and Richard de Redvers, Earl of Devon (father of Baldwin).

1155/56   2nd regnal year of Henry II Confirming the possession of Godshill
          Church to Lyra Abbey as agreed with William Fitz Osbern.

Pope Lucius III by letter confirmed his assent to the appropriation of Godshiil Church to Lyra Abbey as patron.

1195   Confirming the possession of Godshill Church to Pope Celestine
during
          period of excommunication. Pope Celestine III by letter confirmed his
          assent to the appropriation of Godshill Church to Lyra Abbey as
patron.

Pope Innocent III by letter confirmed his assent to the appropriation of Godshill Church to Lyra as patron.

1200   To Walter de Heyno, Stenbury Manor. Permitre land 5 feet in width and as much in depth as required for making a moat around the Manor House.

1200   To Walter de Heyno Confirmation by Thomas de Aula of a grant by his mother Emma of a piece of land at Stenbury Down.

1216   William Earl of Devon (on behalf of Henry III in his 1st regnal year) confirmed to the Abbey of Lyra all the possessions including glebe lands and tithes of all the Churches on the Isle of Wight previously so appropriated including Godshill.

William de Heyno of Stenbury Manor: granted (for a consideration of 2 marks paid by Robert le Hayward, Chaplain to the monks of Carisbrooke Priory) a rent of 4 shillings due on a tenement in Carisbrooke, and renounced his claim to 16d rent due to him on another tenement in Carisbrooke.

1261/77   Exchange of lands between Isabella de Fortibus and the Monks of Carisbrooke Priory. Witnesses to the deed included Johanne Brigg of Bridge Court, and the Lords of the manors of Brook & Standen Manor.

1304   William de Godshill (Rector) and William de Heyno were required to repair the King's Chapel at Swanston, by decision of a Court of Enquiry. This was because the payment for the burial of Lucy de Quereu French at Carisbrooke was not of appropriate value, being a beast of second quality.

Edward II (in return for a fine paid by the Abbot of Lyra) gave licence for the appropriation to it of Godshill Church.

1314   Edward II Letter from Royal Court urging the Bishop of Winchester to assent to the appropriation of Godshill Church including glebe to the Abbot of Lyra.

1315   Queen Isabel, wife of Edward II, Letter urging the Bishop of Winchester to assent to the appropriation of Godshill Church including glebe to the Abbot of Lyra.

1315   Letter from Archbishop of Canterbury to Bishop of Winchester urging him to expedite the appropriation of Godshill Church to the Abbot of Lyra. The monks had not been guilty of buying or trying to buy preferments or practising simony.

1345   Edward III ordered those in charge of the defences of the Isle of Wight to cease exacting from Carisbrooke Priory the provision of four Knights with horses and other contributions for the defence of the Island including the Church of Godshill.

1444   Record of the handing over by the Crown of the Churches including Godshill (originally granted to William Fitz Osbern) to Johannes Bexhingham Prior of Sheen Abbey.

BIBLIOGRAPHY
(as prepared by JVJ, but italics added by Editor)

The History of the Isle of Wight *   Sir Richard Worsley
(1781, re-published 1975)

The Oglander Memoirs

Portrait of the Isle of Wight   L. Wilson

Ward Lock Red Guide of the Isle of Wight

Guides to Godshill Church *   *by P R H Bartlett &HM Worsley*
by Capt HAM Worsley 1935 11th edition

Isle of Wight Villages   P. Sibley

Discovery of the Isle of Wight   P. Sibley

Insula Vectis   S F H

A Picture of the Isle of Wight   H P W

A Short Account of the Geology of the Isle of Wight

A Shell Guide to the Isle of Wight

The Hearth Tax for the Isle of Wight

Water and Windmills in Hampshire & Isle of Wight

Domesday Book - Hampshire

Quarr Abbey 1131-1531   SFH

The Church Vestry Records

Churches of the Isle of Wight *   Margaret Green

Asterisk * denotes that JVJ owned a copy of these works and it is clear that he drew significantly on them and would have wished to acknowledge that fact.

ACKNOWLEDGMENTS
ABOUT THE EDITORS

The Revd Michael Stone MA LLB is JVJ's son-in-law. He has qualifications in History, Theology and Law. Now semi-retired, he is Honorary Secretary of the Suffolk Local History Council. He disclaims any knowledge of Island History, or indeed relationship with the former Vicar of All Saints Godshill of the same surname, but he cherishes memories of his visits to Godshill in the thirty years prior to 2000. He did the major work of editing.

The Revd John Merrick Ryder BA (Hons.), an immigrant from the Colonies and Incumbent of Godshill from 1995, who took a special interest in the history of the church, using it as an example in the lecturing of Church History.

Ralph Abbott, Esq., local businessman and Parish Treasurer for many years, close friend and support of Millicent and Vincent Jenkins during their retirement on the Island, and a local historian.

Dr Paul Tolley, Historian & Librarian, a parishioner.